San Francisco Bay

Discovery and Colonization, 1769–1776

San Francisco Bay

Discovery and Colonization, 1769-1776

BY THEODORE E. TREUTLEIN

CALIFORNIA HISTORICAL SOCIETY

San Francisco 1968

©1968 by the California Historical Society

Special Publication No. 42
Library of Congress Card No. 68-8167

Designed by Adrian Wilson

Printed in the United States of America

Distributed by Lane Magazine & Book Company, Menlo Park, California, 94025
Society members should order directly from the Society.

This work is dedicated to the memory of Herbert Eugene Bolton and Charles Edward Chapman, great teachers and eminent scholars, intellectual explorers and discoverers in the historical archives of Ibero-Americana.

Preface

It has been said that sooner or later anyone living in the Bay Area will attempt to write a book about it, or about San Francisco Bay. Whether or not this be true, when I moved to Berkeley from San Diego, the place of my birth, to begin graduate work in history at the University of California, I immediately became interested in the Bay as a wonderful creation of nature and as an environmental factor influencing social and economic development. The thesis I wrote as part of the Masters program was entitled "Early Explorations of San Francisco Bay" (1930).

Work on the doctorate took me away from that local history theme. However, the present work is distantly related to my first plunge into graduate study. After teaching a History of California course at San Francisco State College for many years—among the several courses which I have given there—I distinctly remember that in about the mid-1950's I began to feel a sense of surprise about the great amount of special interest displayed by local people in the subject of San Francisco's Spanish beginnings.

Yet it may be that such special interest surrounds all local history anywhere, in any time period. Perhaps it is literally true that for most of us "local history" is the gateway to more generalized history, and that, therefore, it is quite appropriate for history buffs to develop an identification with this or that interpretation of their historical background. With respect to the theme treated here, one finds Serra people and Anza people; Moraga people and Richardson people. The debates about the meaning of the mission system, its values, virtues, deficiencies, are notorious, especially in such academic disciplines as sociology, anthropology, and history.

Sometimes the editorial policy of a great newspaper gets its sheet involved in a controversy over historical interpretation. In the case of one metropolitan paper in the Bay Region, any of its writers who refers to "de Anza" must mindlessly, apparently, name him as the "founder of San Francisco." In times past, history has on occasion become a press agent's dream. As true local history knowledge has become more widely disseminated there are hopeful indications that truth is preferred to fiction. We may never again, for instance, have a Portolá celebration such as the one in 1909 during which "Commander Portolá" was sailed into San Francisco Bay in a mock-up "galleon," though as most people know the original Portolá traveled to the vicinity of the later San Francisco on horse or mule-back.

Those who undertake to write "local history" inevitably must feel at least some sense of crusading spirit; they want the "truth" to prevail. The serious student should, without being pretentious, master the source materials as well as the general literature of his subject. Only then can he attempt to relate his story with hoped-for fidelity. As he tries to correct and revise the work of previous writers he must humbly recognize that later someone will critically review his own work.

In this study the story of San Francisco's beginnings is presented as a narrative including free quotations from the documents to form an integral whole. The participants in the story are in this way allowed to speak for themselves. Perhaps through this method we come as close to "oral history" as we can get at this distance in time from the events. However, it must also be recognized that local history cannot be truly local unless a sense of perspective allows us to define its boundaries. From the point of view of the Spanish authorities the establishment of a presidio and mission on the shores of San Francisco Bay was a part of their developing Empire. When we appreciate this fact we can study the "local doings" without giving them a false emphasis. Indeed, the Eighteenth Century explorers and colonizers were really quite humble, hard-working servants of their nation. They had their feelings, but they were not ostentatious.

My first opportunity to work directly on this approach to local history came in the Fall of 1966 with the commencement of a half-year sabbatical leave. In The Bancroft Library I first worked through the entire file of the California Historical Society *Quarterly*, and the Index to the *Quarterly* was of inestimable value in allowing a quick search to be made for information bearing on the period under study. In addition, I reread everything I had read for the M.A. thesis, but very much in addition.

I have taken no translations or interpretations for granted, even when these have been offered by persons whose scholarship I positively revere, particularly that of Herbert Eugene Bolton, and have always gone to the Ms sources to settle, when possible, moot points.

The marvelous microfilm rolls and the excellent reading machines allow the modern scholar to search through piles of *legajos* which were photographed for the library by photographic teams working in Spain, Mexico, and elsewhere. And the Bolton *Guide* and the Chapman *Catalogue*, plus many typescript transcripts of documents in the Bolton Papers, provide the modern investigator in this field with a distinct advantage over the "old California hands" who did a remarkably faithful job in describing what happened here during the Spanish and Mexican periods.

Although the specialist in California History may find the story of San Francisco's beginnings a many-times told tale, even the specialist may appreciate being able to read about it in brief compass. Hopefully, the present work will provide the reader and the specialist with a direct access, often through the words of the participants themselves, to a solid understanding of why and how Spain established her dominion on the shores of San Francisco Bay.

Since the research for this venture in local history was accomplished mainly within the friendly atmosphere of The Bancroft Library, it is a pleasure for me to express particular thanks to Dr. John Barr Tompkins, Head, Public Services, and to the Reference Librarians Mr. Cecil L. Chase, Miss Irene Moran, and Mrs. Linda Schieber, to Library Assistant Mrs. Alma Compton, and to Microfilm Librarian, Mrs. Vivian C. Fisher, and to the hard-working pages, all of whom were unfailingly courteous and helpful in assisting me in finding the materials I needed to use.

Contents

APPENDIXES

NOTE ON THE FOOTNOTES

Permission has been granted by the University of California Press to use
the various passages in this work quoted from the translations of Professor
Herbert Eugene Bolton. The Academy of American Franciscan History
has granted permission to quote from the *Writings of Junípero Serra*, edited
by Antonine Tibesar, O.F.M., and the Franciscan Fathers of California
through the Office of the Provincial have granted permission to quote from
Maynard J. Geiger, O.F.M., *The Life and Times of Fray Junípero Serra,
O.F.M.* The co-operation of these organizations is gratefully acknowledged
by the writer.

I

The Genesis of the Portolá Expedition of 1769

San Francisco had its beginnings in Spanish Empire history, in the latter-day phase of that nation's "defensive expansion", following the Seven Years' War. That great struggle had ended in the Treaty of Paris of 1763; two years later there arrived in New Spain the celebrated Visitor-General Don Joseph de Gálvez, whose role in the California story was to be decisive.[1]

Gálvez was given the primary tasks of increasing the revenues of the empire and of shoring up the defenses of New Spain. In the interest of both these aims he came to the conclusion that Upper California should be occupied. In preparing the groundwork for the occupation, Gálvez stressed the need for defending the empire; the drive into Upper California would be a countermove to a possible foreign settlement on the west coast of North America.

As an immediate approach to the problem of defense Gálvez sent an emissary to present his arguments; his choice of emissary being one Antonio Ricardos, a field-marshal, who was expected to acquaint the First Minister of State to Charles III, the Marqués

---

[1] Herbert Ingram Priestley, *José de Gálvez. Visitor-General of New Spain, 1765–1771* (1916). Charles Edward Chapman appreciated the "Spanish Empire approach" to California history better than most. See his *The Founding of Spanish California, etc.* (1916); *A History of California: The Spanish Period* (1921); also the marvelously succinct and well-documented paper, "The Founding of San Francisco", in *The Pacific Ocean in History. Papers and Addresses Presented at the Panama-Pacific Historical Congress Held at San Francisco, Berkeley and Palo Alto, California. July 19–23, 1915.* H. Morse Stephens and Herbert E. Bolton, eds. (1917). Irving Berdine Richman, *California Under Spain and Mexico, 1835–1847* (1911) is also useful for documentation and maps.

de Grimaldi, with the need for taking possession of Monterey, owing to foreign attempts at establishment on the Pacific Coast.[2] Don Ricardos was listed as a passenger aboard the ship *Dragon* when she sailed out of Vera Cruz on the 24th of May, 1767, and presumably carried out his mission.[3] There seems little doubt that it was Gálvez who conceived the idea of founding Spanish settlements in Upper California (part of the *Peninsula of Californias*, in the language of that day), that Ricardos went to Spain to influence the Court in favor of this project through Minister Grimaldi, and that Gálvez did receive Crown support for the venture.

A complete documentation of the apparent causal relationship between Gálvez' plans and Grimaldi's support of them is lacking, but the latter did follow upon the former, and in due time an extremely important despatch from Grimaldi, supportive of Gálvez' views, reached the Viceroy of Mexico at a time when Gálvez had already left the capital and was on his way to San Blas on the west coast of New Spain. The Viceroy sent a courier after Gálvez who was overtaken two days out of Guadalajara; the courier carried a letter from the Viceroy, dated April 30, 1768, and also the Grimaldi despatch. These messages were all that Gálvez needed to support his decision to occupy Upper California.

Minister Grimaldi had written: "The Russians have several times made attempts to open a route to America and have recently carried out their intention through navigating in the northern part of the Pacific. We are certain they have succeeded and that they have reached the mainland, but we do not know in which degree [of latitude] they have made their landing. [It is] apparently a place inhabited by savages with whom they fought, with the resulting death of three hundred Russians.

---

[2] Priestley, *op. cit.*, p. 245 ff. See Appendix, this work, for the complete document entitled "Plan for the Erection of a Government and General Commandancy". The "Plan" may be studied in its microfilm copy, Bancroft Library, *Archivo General de la Nación* (Mexico) [hereinafter, *AGN*], Provincias Internas, 154. In the microfilm the document terminates with the names, "El Marques de Croix" = "Don José de Gálvez", apparently to indicate that they were co-signers. In the document, it should be noted, the Dutch and English are mentioned, along with the Russians, as a source of concern to the Spanish Crown.

[3] *Archivo General de Indias* (Seville) [hereinafter, *AGI*], Audiencia de Guadalajara, 417, Reel #353, 30 May 1767, Mexico. Croix to Arriaga. Microfilm, Bancroft Library.

"A consequence of this we believe is that they will make new expeditions in continuation of their supposed discoveries in those parts, their belief being that in this way they would acquire a new branch of commerce which they flatter themselves would have great value despite the great distance to it overland, because of its nearness to the *Vesen* [*sic*], a sea which may be ice-free in those places, and because of their uncertainty of the distance to California, the only country explored in that region.

"The King has ordered me to inform Your Grace of the danger so that the governor named for California can be made alert and be given instructions with regard to the watchfulness and concern he should exercise in observing the attempts the Russians are able to make there, thwarting them however possible and providing immediate information of everything to Your Grace for his Majesty.

God keep Your Grace many years, etc."[4]

Gálvez continued his journey to San Blas and began its construction as a naval base. His arrival there is dated 13 May; three days later, fired by his own zeal and now by the Crown's orders, he convened a junta where were formulated the plans for occupying Monterey. Then he wrote a letter, dated May 20, and told the Viceroy what had transpired in the junta. The letter to the Viceroy is a letter of transmittal for the junta proceedings. Both documents are of fundamental importance for an understanding of the program of exploration and colonization which was to follow.

The letter of transmittal should be considered first, because it provides the setting for the plan which had been developed in the junta. Visitor-General Gálvez wrote: "In fulfillment of his Majesty's order communicated to you on January 23 by the

---

[4] *AGN*, Reales Cedulas, Vols. 91(2)–93(1), Reel #51, El Pardo, 23 January 1768, Grimaldi to Croix. Microfilm, Bancroft Library. This document is based upon *AGI*, Papeles de Estado, 86, Roll I *in* reel #5281, microfilm, Bancroft, Herriára [the Spanish Minister in Russia] to Grimaldi, Moscow 31/20 November 1767. See Appendix, p. 107 for the last page of this coded message. Incongruous as it may seem from a geographical point of view, the sea referred to as *Vesen* is probably Baffin Bay, transliterated from *Bafins*, as, for example, in the document of 1766 wherein is expressed concern that a passage may be found by other powers through North America to the South Sea [the Pacific]; Bolton Papers, Alta California, Item #80.

Marqués de Grimaldi [January 23, 1768, dated at El Pardo], concerning repeated attempts which the Russians have made to open communication with North America, and in consequence also of what you command in your letter of April, inclosing a copy of the above-mentioned order, and recalling to mind the many conversations and reflections which we have previously had concerning the supreme importance and utility of taking possession of the port of Monterey and establishing there a presidio, I am obeying your order to take such measures as I deem fitting for reaching that place by land or sea. As you leave me discretion for the fulfillment of this order, it has seemed to me both fitting and necessary that I should inform you from here of the resolution which it was thought proper to take in this weighty matter."[5]

The San Blas meeting is then described in full in the document: "Junta Held at San Blas by the Visitador General Joseph de Gálvez, May 16, 1768, at which the plan to occupy the Puerto de Monterrey[6] by expeditions by land and sea was formulated in accordance with the Royal Order of his Majesty, Don Carlos III, January 23, 1768.

"In the harbor and new settlement of San Blas of the Kingdom of Nueva Galicia on the coast of the South Sea on the sixteenth day of May of the year 1768, the Most Illustrious Señor Don Joseph de Gálvez, of His Majesty's Supreme Council of the Indies, Quartermaster General of the Army, Visitador General of the Tribunals and of the Royal Treasury of these Kingdoms, empowered with fullest authority by the Most Excellent Señor Marqués de Croix, Viceroy, Governor and Captain General of this Nueva España, summoned to his quarters in the government buildings, the Engineer, Don Miguel Costansó; the Comandante of the Navy & this Harbor, Don Manuel Ribero Cordero; Don Antonio Fabeau de Quesada, Professor of Mathematics, and experienced in the Navigation of these Seas and those of the Philippine Islands; and Don Vicente Vila, Pilot of the Royal Armada of His Majesty on the

---

[5] Priestley, *op. cit.*, p. 246.

[6] The original spelling of Monterey was Monterrey. In this work the name will be rendered with either one *r* or with two *r*s, depending upon the form being followed in a given document. In the body of the text the modern form, *Monterey*, will be used.

Atlantic Ocean, and designated as Chief Pilot of the vessels that ply this Pacific Ocean.

"A Royal Order of His Majesty sent by His Excellency the Marqués de Grimaldi, of the Council & First Secretary of State, under date of the twenty-third of January of this year to the Most Excellent Señor, Marqués de Croix, Viceroy of this Kingdom, having been read to them, which imparting definite knowledge of the attempts which the Russians have made to facilitate their communication with this America, warned His Excellency to dispatch instructions and orders to the Governor of California to observe from there the designs of that nation and to frustrate them as far as possible; and the Junta was also informed of the official letter & order of His Majesty, a copy of which His Excellency the Viceroy had passed on to the Señor Visitador General so that, being fully acquainted with it and putting into practice the former plans of occupancy with a Presidio at Puerto de Monterrey, situated on the Great Ocean, on the west coast of California, he might adopt those measures he deems most expedient in order to explore by land and by sea so important a harbor, sending an engineer so that, having taken exact observations and having made a map of the harbor, the useful project of establishing ourselves at that place may be accomplished.

"Above all, the Most Illustrious Señor, Don Joseph de Gálvez, added that since there will arrive in a very short while at this harbor of San Blas the two new brigantines, *San Carlos* and *El Príncipe*, which have transported to the harbor of Guaymas in Sonora the infantry destined for the expedition against the Seri, Pima and Apache Indians, and at the same time since the sloop called *La Sinaloa* and the packet boat *La Concepción* are anchored here to make the voyage to California, and since the new bark now in the ship-yards is in condition to be launched by the beginning of July, according to the reports of the Comandante Don Manuel Ribero and the Master of Construction, it is the intention of the Visitador General, with the approval of all concerned, if the present season is favorable for undertaking the voyage for the aforementioned harbor of Monterrey, to make known at once his orders to this end with the idea of hastening so important an expedition and to adopt,

as soon as he arrives in the Californias, measures most in con-
formity with the reports & the knowledge he will there acquire, so
that at the proper time, if it be possible, another expedition or
journey by land may be undertaken with the same purpose,
namely: to discover and take possession of the aforementioned
harbor of Monterrey, by means of a Presidio.

"These points were intelligently discussed and weighed at length
and in view of all the facts set forth and others which have been
considered, and with the concurrence of opinion of all the members
of this Junta, it was agreed that the most favorable time for the
voyage to Monterrey, whether from this harbor of San Blas or
from Cape San Lucas in California, is from the coming months of
June and July until the September equinox, because that is the season during which the equinoctial winds blowing toward the Pole
rule in these seas, which winds are most favorable for making the
voyage and attaining latitude 38° or 39° and thus reach the aforementioned harbor of Monterrey which is located in 37° less ten
minutes.

"At the same time it was also agreed that it would be most important to undertake an entry or search by land, at the proper sea-
sons, from the missions to the north of California, so that both
expeditions might unite at the same harbor of Monterrey, and by
means of the observations made by one and the other they might
acquire once and for all complete knowledge and in this wise aid
greatly the founding of a presidio and settlement at that place
which is truly the most advantageous for protecting the entire
west coast of California and the other coasts of the southern part
of this continent, against any attempts by the Russians or any
northern nation.

"In consequence of all this, the Illustrious Señor Don Joseph de
Gálvez, with the approval of all, agreed & resolved that there be
made ready at once all the necessary supplies of provision, rigging,
sails and whatever else is thought useful and indispensable to be
put aboard the two aforementioned new brigantines which are to
undertake the voyage to the harbor of Monterrey by leaving the
coast and the chain of islands behind and undertaking the voyage
on the high seas, thus to reach the proper latitude as far as the
winds of the season will permit so as not to experience the delays,

misfortunes and sicknesses which were suffered by the expeditions of Don Sebastián Vizcaíno, & others made during the last two centuries.

"And in order that proper means may be adopted to assure as far as it is humanly possible the happy outcome of this enterprise, the aforementioned brigantines are to be fitted out immediately upon their arrival at this harbor of San Blas, so that by the middle of next June they may sail for Cape San Lucas where they are to receive instructions from the Illustrious Señor Visitador General, and begin their voyage to their destination.

"One brigantine is to be under command of Chief Pilot Don Vicente Vila, who will take with him as second pilot one from among those now serving in these waters; the other is to be in command of Don Antonio Faveau with a second class pilot. The same Don Antonio shall also go as engineer, being versed in that profession, so as to aid Don Miguel Costansó under whose orders the Visitador General will place the soldiers and people he is to assign to the brigantines so as to assure this reconnaissance and the founding of the presidio & settlement that will be established in the aforesaid Puerto de Monterrey; for it should not be difficult to take possession of some advantageous site there, granting that the natives of that place show themselves as peaceful and friendly as they have on other occasions.

"Finally, there is left to the care & resolution of the Illustrious Señor, Don Joseph de Gálvez, the examination and decision on his arrival in California [the Peninsula] whether it be possible to send at the proper time persons satisfactory to him with the corresponding party and detachment which are to make the entry or journey by land to the aforementioned Puerto de Monterrey, for it will always be most prudent and advantageous to bring together the two expeditions at that place.

"Thus it was decided and His Illustriousness signed with the others who were present at this Junta and conference."[7]

There can be no doubt that the decision by Gálvez to take possession of Upper California through the planting there of settle-

---

[7] *The Spanish Occupation of California: . . . Junta or Council Held at San Blas, May 16, 1768 . . .* Douglas S. Watson and Thomas Workman Temple II, translators (San Francisco; Grabhorn, 1934). Gálvez always signed his first name Joseph, not José.

ments was dictated primarily by "defense of Empire" considerations. Don Gaspar de Portolá, Governor of Lower California, was chosen to head the enterprise, but Gálvez also included a program of mission-founding, to carry out a general Crown policy of spreading the Faith, because the experience of Spain's administrators had proved without question that the mission was an excellent institution for the pacification of the frontier.[8] The secular function of the mission was probably as important as its religious function in the history of Spanish frontier development. Since "pacification" of the Indians was equated in the minds of the Spanish with conversion to Christianity of these "heathen" people, the mission had a great civilizing purpose including, it should be mentioned in passing, its special economic importance.

The use of soldiers, missionaries, and ultimately secular colonists in effectuating Empire expansion was based upon Sixteenth, Seventeenth, and early Eighteenth Century experience. Had Visitor Gálvez used only the military arm of the state in beginning the Upper California program, he would in truth have violated the tradition and practical experience accumulated during the colonial period in New Spain.

Thus, when Gálvez made reference to the "holy" or "sacred" expedition as he did in a letter to Father Palóu on 9 January 1769, after bidding farewell to the ship, *San Carlos*, and when he informed Captain Portolá that the main object of the expedition was to spread the Faith among the heathen, he voiced a deeply felt reli-

---

[8] Theodore E. Treutlein, "The Economic Regime of the Jesuit Missions in Eighteenth Century Sonora," *Pacific Historical Review*, VIII (September, 1939); and, in general, Herbert E. Bolton, "The Mission as a Frontier Institution in the Spanish-American Colonies," *American Historical Review*, XXIII (October, 1917).

In addition to the author's own conclusions on this subject of the role of the mission there is, for example, the opinion of Maynard J. Geiger, O.F.M., *The Life and Times of Fray Junípero Serra, O.F.M., etc.* (Washington; Academy of American Franciscan History, 1959), 2 vols., in I, p. 208, where Father Geiger states: "Many documents, such as the instructions issued to Portolá by Gálvez, insist that the principal object was to extend the Catholic faith among the pagans of the territory. But . . . [there is] clear evidence that the occasion and the purpose in Spain's taking Upper California was not primarily the spreading of the Gospel or the conversion of the Indian but the thwarting of Russia. Once the land had been secured, it had to be held for the same reason and the Spaniards there were to use Spain's traditional means of pacific conquest—namely, the Christianization and civilizing of the Indians through the Spanish mission system . . ." See also text, pp. 46–48, on the question of the "foreign" threat.

gious sentiment, but he did not refer to a religious crusade. The crusade, if such it may be called, was for the defense of Empire, and in this the mission was to play its part in Upper California as it had already done in other parts of the Kingdom of New Spain.[9]

Because the Society of Jesus had been suppressed in Spain and

---

[9] The writer has been able to discover only one use of the expression, "sacred expedition", in the documents having to do with the Portolá expedition. This is rather surprising in view of the currency which this expression has gained, even among secular writers. The expression, in the singular, was used by Gálvez in a letter dated at La Paz [Baja California], 9 January 1769, addressed to Father Francisco Palóu telling the latter of the departure of the *San Carlos*. There we find " . . . Vá saliendo el Sn. Carlos de este Puerto p.ª la *Sta. Expedicion,* y lleva provisiones y repuestos para un año . . . " [Italics, T.E.T.] Transcript, Bancroft Library. *Mexico, Museo Nacional, Papeles de Lancaster-Jones, Documentos relativos á las misiones de Californias,* I.

In the first paragraph of his instructions to Portolá, dated at Cape San Lucas, 20 Feburary 1769, Gálvez makes it plain that spiritual conquest would directly serve the Crown. He wrote: "Considering that the main object of this expedition is that of spreading the Faith among the heathen who live north of this peninsula by the peaceful means of establishing missions which will effect a spiritual conquest in the said ports of San Diego and Monterrey, and in other places in between which now will be opened, and can be controlled most effectively through requiring reductions, *and through them to establish the domination of the King, Our Master,* the said Governor will prepare as soon as possible, etc." [italics, T.E.T.]. For the Gálvez instructions to Portolá see *AGI,* Aud. de Guad., 417, Reel #353, microfilm, Bancroft Library.

What might be called the secular form of the above sentiment is expressed in the "Plan", see above, footnote #2. In this document, in their arguments in favor of their proposal, these high officials frequently show the inextricable relationship which existed in their minds between *statecraft* (i.e., gaining territory, riches, honor for the Crown; maintaining the security of the Empire) and *religion* (i.e., converting heathen, conquering souls for the Creator, in reward for which "God is allotting to the Crown of Spain the Richest Empires of the Universe"). The sole aim of their Plan, they declare, "is to promote the public Interests of the King and the State in an establishment which, besides the urgent necessity of effecting it (i.e., because of the "Russian menace") will be very advantageous in a short time" (i.e., through financial or economic gains to the Crown).

Later in the year 1768 a despatch was sent from San Lorenzo, Spain, to the Viceroy in Mexico, 18 October, wherein it is stated that the King has received word through a letter of 28 May [1768] concerning the steps being planned by Gálvez to thwart the Russian program of expansion through establishing a presidio at Monterey. The King, says the despatch, had expressed impatience at not receiving further information concerning the progress being made in such an important matter. Nothing is said in this despatch about religious motivation or about the mission system. See *AGI,* Aud. de Guad. 417, Reels 353–368, microfilm, Bancroft Library.

Finally, when Father Francisco Palóu composed his famous multi-volume *Noticias de la Nueva California,* translated and edited by H. E. Bolton as *Historical Memoirs of New California* [hereinafter, Palóu, *Historical Memoirs*], he makes no reference whatsoever to the "Sacred Expedition" or expeditions, by such a title. Yet the Gálvez letter of 9 January 1769 was addressed to Palóu, as was also another letter of 20 February 1769, and in these Gálvez makes reference to the "holy purpose of our undertaking". See Palóu, *ibid.,* IV, Letter IV.

in the Spanish dominions in 1767, Gálvez could not call upon Jesuits to serve in the California venture, even had they been his choice. The Franciscans of the San Fernando College were now chosen, and Father Junípero Serra was named to serve as the father president of the Upper California missions. Six weeks prior to the time when Gálvez and Serra had a personal meeting to talk over future plans, Gálvez had sent a letter bearing the date September 15, 1768 to Father Serra. The Visitor-General's words were as follows: "It is quite proper that each religious order should invoke the protection of its own saints, and especially must we remember the seraphic saint, Our Father San Francisco . . .

"We have seen how, in happy prophecy, the old explorers gave the names of some of them to the principal points on the coast above and below Monterey. The port where one of the new missions is now to be established they called San Diego, and that appellation must not be changed. To another fine harbor, situated in thirty-eight and one-half degrees, they gave the name of the glorious patriarch San Francisco, and we must not change this very appropriate title, for after a foothold is once gained in Monterey it must be the first mission to follow; and our Father, being so beloved of God, will facilitate the establishment by means of his powerful intercession. Let the intervening mission be called San Buenaventura as a guaranty of good fortune, and let those that may be founded afterward take the names of other saints of the order.

"We must not take away the name of San Carlos from the port or from the town to be founded at Monterey, for it is the good-omened name of our beloved sovereign, of the Prince of the Asturias, and of the present Viceroy of New Spain. Nevertheless, the titular saint of that church must be the patriarch Señor San Joseph, because the present expedition has been undertaken under his special patronage; but my saint will not be offended if the temple having his appellation is small, for he is very humble . . . and besides, he already has on the Peninsula [of Baja California] two missions commended to his protection."[10]

---

[10] Letter quoted in H. E. Bolton, *Fray Juan Crespi, Missionary Explorer on the Pacific Coast: 1769–1774* (Berkeley, 1927), xxxii–xxxiii. In Father Palóu's *Life of Serra* there is related a charming incident quite famous in California lore, that Serra asked Gálvez,

when the latter was naming missions to be founded: "Is there to be no mission in honor of Our Holy Father, St. Francis?", and Gálvez is supposed to have replied: "Let him find the port bearing his name and he will have his mission there." Geiger, *op. cit.*, I, pp. 204–205, discusses this subject and points out that Palóu could not have been reporting a conversation because the missions had already been named before Serra and Gálvez met. However, the question asked by Serra, says Geiger, could have been posed in a letter, since "it appears from [Gálvez'] answer that such a question was asked." [The "answer" referred to here is quoted above, p. 10 in the text; however, there is no documentation in the Geiger account of a Serra letter wherein the "question" might have been put.]

There is a letter from the Franciscan Guardian, Rafael Verger, to the Fiscal, Manuel Lanz de Casafonda, 22 August 1771, which contains a summary of the three classes of missions listed by Gálvez which would extend from Lower California to the north. In this list San Francisco is not mentioned, though "Sn. Francisco de Boija" [*sic*] for Lower California is included. In M 1847 (from MS. Add. 13974, British Museum), Bancroft Library.

2

The Transfer of the Name "San Francisco" to the Bay and Its Environs

The mention of San Francisco Bay by Visitor Gálvez, it should be stated at once, came out of his knowledge of early explorations in which a bay or port of San Francisco is named and located, but this was not the present San Francisco Bay. San Francisco was first used as a place name in Upper California by Sebastián Rodríguez Cermeño, Captain of the Manila Galleon, the *San Agustín*, on the 7th of November, 1595. On that date "the Captain landed . . . took possession of the land and port, which he named the bay of San Francisco. Fray Francisco de la Concepción of the Order of Barefoot Franciscans baptized it."[11] It is now known that this name was given to the bay nowadays called Drake's Bay, and it was to this name and port that Gálvez made reference in his letter to Father Serra.[12]

We do not know why Cermeño gave the name San Francisco to his bay of refuge, only that the bay proved a false refuge, for his ship was there destroyed. When he departed the bay in a make-shift long-boat, the date was 8 December, and he passed close to the Farallon Islands on the mainland side. The day was cloudy

---

[11] Henry R. Wagner, "The Voyage to California of Sebastian Rodriguez Cermeño in 1595", *California Historical Society Quarterly* [hereinafter, *CHSQ*], III, No. 1 (April, 1924).

[12] See the Cabrera Bueno *derrota*, Appendix, this volume.

and there was a strong wind. "He sailed a great deal . . . without discovering in all this distance anything worth noting down."[13]

But Cermeño had left a name, and in later years this name was incorporated in the navigation handbook written by J. Gónzalez Cabrera Bueno, published in 1734, wherein the author described the coastal ship's course (*derrota*) from Cape Mendocino to Acapulco.[14] Cabrera Bueno, who was always referred to in this way in the travel accounts later, may have been the source of information for Gálvez' reference to San Francisco, though Gálvez probably had other sources as well.[15] In the navigation handbook the "Port of San Francisco" could be recognized from its three white cliffs (*barrancas blancas*), and in the middle area by an estuary with a good entrance without any breakers; entering it one would find friendly Indians and easily obtained fresh water.[16]

Thus, when Visitor Gálvez was organizing the expedition to occupy Monterey, which became known as the Portolá expedition, he had through his reference to San Francisco accomplished two things, one of them direct and specific, the other, accidental. The direct result of the Gálvez reference was that an order had been given and would sooner or later have to be carried out, thus fortifying Father Serra's great interest in a mission "on the port of Our Father, San Francisco", or even as noted, perhaps supplying the idea. The accidental aspect arose mainly from the circumstance

---

[13] Halleck F. Raup, "The Delayed Discovery of San Francisco Bay," *CHSQ*, XXVII, No. 4 (December, 1948).

[14] Appendix, Cabrera Bueno *derrota*.

[15] Miguel Venegas in his famous *Noticias de la California* . . . (1757) included in an Appendix the "Narrative of the voyage of Captain Sebastian Vizcaino in the year 1602, for surveying the outward or western coast of California on the South Sea". This was based upon the account in Juan de Torquemada, *Monarchia Indiana* (1615) which was quite a rare work in Venegas' time even though a new edition (Madrid, 1725) had appeared. In the Torquemada account used by Venegas there is reference to Vizcaíno's arrival at the Port of San Francisco, 7 January 1603, and the desire of Francisco Bolaños (pilot with Vizcaíno as he had been with Cermeño) to go ashore and search for "a great quantity of wax and several chests of silk" which had been landed there from the ill-fated *San Agustín*. Thus, Gálvez could have read about the Port of San Francisco both in Torquemada and Venegas, as well as in Cabrera Bueno. The "explorers" to whom he refers must have been Cermeño and Vizcaíno.

[16] Cabrera Bueno based his description of the port on the words of Bolaños. See Wagner, article cited in note 11, above, and the *derrota*.

that Cabrera Bueno's port and the great, as yet undiscovered, San Francisco Bay, were near enough to each other to become related in the minds of the earliest explorers. Gradually then, after the discovery of the inner bay, the name San Francisco was transferred to its present site, when it became obvious that there were two harbors or ports, and that one was truly different from the other.

It would be convenient to have an official document proclaiming this transfer of names, but none such exists. The change of names simply came about through usage, and one cannot even state exactly when this kind of transfer occurred. Probably the new identification was completed by 1775. In this way it happened that a name, San Francisco, first applied in 1595 by Cermeño to the presently called Drake's Bay, and then "popularized" among those schooled in Eighteenth Century geographical knowledge by the Cabrera Bueno *Guide to Navigation*, ultimately became the title of the great inland bay.

3

The Discovery and First Exploration of San Francisco Bay: 1769

The great inner Bay of San Francisco remained undiscovered by Europeans until it was first seen by members of the Portolá land expedition, probably by a party of scouts led by Sergeant José Francisco Ortega on 1 November 1769. Captain Gaspar de Portolá's expedition made its march to the Bay area almost exactly two hundred and twenty-seven years after the voyage of Juan Rodríguez Cabrillo, the first European who could have seen the entrance to the Bay, but who passed it some miles at sea without sighting it, except possibly as part of what appeared to be a continuous coastline.[17]

On first thought it may seem curious that mariners sailing in some two hundred voyages, most of them heading south, failed to

---

[17] After Cabrillo had come his pilot, Ferrelo. Then followed Drake, Gali, Unamuno, Cermeño [as noted], Teixeira, Vizcaíno, and Lope de Ulloa. Also after 1565 there occurred the annual voyage of the Manila Galleon, sailing south along the coast. The galleon approached the coast either above or close to the latitude of San Francisco Bay. Among those named here, Gali and Cermeño were galleon skippers. A list of these navigators with an analysis of their voyages relative to the entrance of the Bay is found in the H. F. Raup article, *op. cit.*

Francis Drake is believed by some to have discovered and entered San Francisco Bay. A recent article on the Drake question, which includes important commentary on the "Drake Plate", is found in Walter A. Starr, "Drake Landed in San Francisco Bay in 1579", *CHSQ*, Vol. XLI, No. 3 (September, 1962), but the arguments offered are not acceptable to this writer as proof of Drake's discovery of an entrance into the Bay. R. F. Heizer, *Francis Drake and the California Indians* (Berkeley; U.C. Press, 1947) is quite convincing on the point that Drake did, indeed, sojourn in the bay now known as Drake's Bay. There is a great literature on the Drake question which is not germane here.

sight the mouth of the Bay when in the latitude of its entrance. However, a brief consideration of the configuration of the coast, questions of visibility owing to weather conditions, the backdrop effect of the East Bay Hills, and the positions of the islands— Alcatraz and Angel—within the Bay, can convince one to accept a contrary view; namely, that it would have been remarkable had the entrance to San Francisco Bay been discovered from the sea. On an approach from the sea one cannot look far through the Bay's entrance until one is within the line between Points Lobos and Bonita, and not even then unless near the shallow "Potato Patch" on the north side. The early century skippers in their wisdom did not hug a forbidding coastline, and it may be convincingly argued that the delayed discovery of the Bay was a tribute to the seamanship of these early navigators.[18]

This brings us to the subject of the actual discovery of the Bay. The Portolá expedition, moving north from San Diego in its attempt to carry out the first phase of the Gálvez program, the discovery and occupation of Monterey Bay, had failed to recognize that place, had passed it to go north, and had made camp, on October 31, 1769, in San Pedro Valley (Linda Mar of modern Pacifica).

When the members of the expedition topped the ridge above San Pedro Valley on Monday afternoon, 30 October, they first saw the great outer San Francisco Bay, now known as the Gulf of the Farallones. This body of water, stretching from Point San Pedro northwest to Point Reyes and including the Farallon Islands, was immediately recognized by the leaders of the expedition to be the Port of San Francisco, as described in the Cabrera Bueno *derrota*, a navigator's view of the coastline.

Engineer Miguel Costansó and Father Juan Crespí both left fairly detailed descriptions of what they saw from the ridge, but it is obvious from the entries in their diaries that their understanding of what they saw was strongly conditioned by what they had previously read in Cabrera's Navigator's Guide. "As soon as we

---

[18] Raup, *op. cit.* This is a definitive article on the subject of the delayed discovery of the Bay. The present writer came to the same conclusion as did Raup concerning the reasons for this delay [M.A. thesis, mentioned in the Preface, this work], but did not develop the subject as completely as has Dr. Raup.

ascended to the summit," wrote Crespí, "we descried a great bay formed by a point of land which runs far out into the open sea and looks like an island. Farther out, about west-northwest from where we stood and a little to the southwest of the point, six or seven white farallones of different sizes were to be seen. Following the coast of the bay to the north some white cliffs are visible, and to the northwest is the mouth of an estuary which seems to penetrate into the land. In view of these signs, and what is stated in the itinerary of the pilot Cabrera Bueno, we came to the recognition of this port; it is that of our Father San Francisco, and we have left that of Monterey behind."[19]

Despite a general agreement that this body of water was, indeed, the Port of San Francisco, and that the Port of Monterey now lay behind them, Commander Portolá decided to send out an exploring party to dispel all doubts concerning their location. The explorers had specific instructions to explore the land for a certain distance— the precise charge being that they should proceed as far as Point Reyes, because that was the actual area where the sea entered the

---

[19] Bolton, *Crespi*. Diary; entry for 31 October 1769 [hereinafter, Crespí *Diary*]. Two forms of the Costansó diary are used in this work; "Diary of Miguel Costansó", ed. by Frederick J. Teggart, *in* Academy of Pacific Coast History, *Publications*, Vol. 2, No. 4 (1911) [hereinafter, Costansó, *Diary*], and a photo-copy and typescripts in the Bolton Papers (Bancroft Library), which appears to be the first form of the diary and which differs in some essential points from the Teggart edition; it also appears not to have been previously cited. This form of the Costansó diary was photographed from Legajo 53, *Biblioteca Nacional* (Mexico) and is referred to hereinafter as Legajo 53. Costansó wrote to Gálvez from San Diego, 7 Feb. 1770, and mentioned his diary which he said: "lacks the introduction and end, which I formed separately, . . . It also lacks being tied and bound up with that of the sea [the diary of the sea voyage to San Diego] which I still have only in rough draft . . . " The appearance of Legajo 53 is exactly as Costansó describes his diary; it lacks an introduction and end. See Bolton Papers, Alta California, Item #90, Folder 19.

In the early diaries Point San Pedro is known as *Angel de la Guardia*, alias *Punta de Almejas*, the latter because of the shell-fish, mussels, found there.

See George Davidson, *The Discovery of San Francisco Bay* (1907), for an interesting discussion of what Davidson thought the explorers saw from Pt. San Pedro. He was certain that the white cliffs and the estuary reported by Crespí [and Costansó] are the ones in the Bolinas area; that the "estuary" was actually the valley which runs from Bolinas Bay to Tomales Bay, rather than "Drake's Estuary" and the white cliffs of Drake's Bay, which the explorers reported sighting and which supported their belief in the accuracy of the Cabrera Bueno description. The point is, of course, not what the explorers saw, but what they thought and believed that they saw. Davidson contends that Pt. Bonita was originally Pt. Bonete, because it resembled a clerical hat.

land, according to Cabrera[20]—and to return to the camp within
three days' time. Under Sergeant Ortega's command the scouts
left camp after Mass, on the Wednesday morning of 1 November.

Meanwhile, the rest of the party camped in the valley which had
a fine, running stream, a large, reed-covered swamp which was also
the sink of the river, and good pasturage for the animals. Nearby
was the beach which they described as the south shore of the Bay
or Port of San Francisco. On the morning of the 2nd of November,
Thursday, immediately after Mass, some of the soldiers, having
secured permission for this, set out on a deer hunt. They apparently moved up the valley and into the eastern ridges, for they returned to camp that night with an exciting story of what they had
seen from the high ground.

Costansó recorded what the hunters reported. "They said that
to the north of the bay they had seen an immense arm of the sea or
estuary, which extended inland as far as they could see, to the
southeast; that they had seen some beautiful plains studded with
trees; and that from the columns of smoke they had noticed all
over the level country, there was no doubt that the land must be
well populated with natives. This ought to confirm us more and
more in the opinion that we were at the port of San Francisco, and
that this was the estuary of which the pilot Cabrera Bueno spoke
[editorialized Costansó]. We had seen its entrance between some
ravines while descending the slope of the bay . . . "

"We conjectured from this information," added Costansó,
"that the explorers would not have been able to reach the shore
visible to the north and therefore could not reconnoiter *La Punta
de los Reyes*, because in the few days they had they could not get
around the estuary whose length was so enlarged upon by the
hunters."[21]

Both Costansó and Crespí believed (as they revealed in their
diaries for 2 November) that the estuary seen by the hunters was

---

[20] Neither Diary (Crespí nor Costansó) makes clear that the explorers were to proceed as far as Pt. Reyes. However, "The Narrative of the Portolá Expedition of 1769–
1770 by Miguel Costansó", ed. by A. Van Hemert-Engert and F. J. Teggart, *in* Acad.
of Pac. Coast Hist., *Publications*, Vol. 1, No. 4 (1910) [hereinafter Costanó's *Narrative*, and Legajo 53], each mention this specific charge to Ortega.

[21] Legajo 53.

the very one described by Cabrera Bueno, and both quoted from Cabrera's *derrota* an excerpt which describes the estuary as entering the land through the middle *barranca*.[22]

This report of the "deer hunters" was the first recorded description of the southern arm of San Francisco Bay. It must remain a matter of speculation as to whether the hunters were, indeed, the first to see it. The surmise is that they were not, and that actually Sergeant Ortega and his scouts probably saw the southern arm of the Bay a day earlier; however, the Ortega report to Commander Portolá could not be made until the evening of the third day, namely, on the 3rd of November.

On the evening of the 3rd, before they reached camp, the Ortega party could be heard firing salutes from their arms. The entire camp was aroused "and kept in a state of great expectation" by the signals, and all went out on the road to meet the explorers. They brought the news that *two days' march from the place at which they had arrived* there was, according to the sign language of the natives, a port with a ship in it. Some members of the party were now convinced that they had reached Monterey, and that the packet ship, *San Jose* was awaiting them in that port. Later, in his polished *Narrative*, Engineer Costansó was to write: "Little importance was attached to this information—obtained by the doubtful means of signs made by the hands and head, which on such occasion take the place of the tongue."[23] Nevertheless, even the remotest possibility that the ship might be there would have to be tested, and this realization became the cause for some further exploration of the Bay during the next few days.

What had the first official explorers under Ortega's command seen and exactly where had they gone during the three days which elapsed from early morning of the 1st of November until the night of 3 November? The answers to these questions cannot be directly given, but must be surmised from pieces of information which may be gleaned from the writings of Ortega, Costansó, Crespí, Portolá, and from certain statements relevant to the questions included in the diaries of later years as written by Fages, Rivera,

[22] Costansó and Crespí diaries, entries for 3 November.
[23] Compare Costansó and Crespí diaries with the Costansó *Narrative*.

Palóu, Font, and Anza. In addition to the literary records there is
an early map prepared by Costansó which must also be considered
in the search for answers.

It is clear enough that when Ortega's party left the San Pedro
Camp there was nowhere for them to go but northward and up.
The valley is a sheltered one, bounded by the sea, sea-cliffs, and
the ridges surrounding the valley. Horsemen could not have proceeded along the beach for any great distance. The direction of Ortega's march was toward the north; for that is where *La Punta de los
Reyes* extended into the sea, which the entire expedition had already seen. In going northward Ortega and his men ascended hills
and ridges and could have sighted the southern arm of San Francisco Bay by mid-morning of the 1st of November, and the most
likely place for this sighting was in the neighborhood of "Fog
Gap", which lies to the east of Mussel Rock. There can be no
doubt that the explorers did sight the southern arm of the Bay
between the 1st and the 3rd; this is stated in the writings of Costansó, Crespí, and Commander Portolá himself.[24] The excitement
about the "port with a ship in it" occupied the attention of the
diarists on the 3rd of November.

The explorers had had great fortune with the weather; no fog
obscured the vision of the scouting party. This convenient information is furnished in the Costansó entry for 12 November, when
it is stated that from the first sighting of the Port of San Francisco
(the afternoon of 30 October) until that day, the expedition had
experienced clear skies and no mist.[25] Thus, the likelihood of a 1st

------

[24] Costansó *Narrative;* Crespí, letter to Palóu, San Diego, 6 February 1770 in
Palóu, *Historical Memoirs;* and the "Diary of Gaspar de Portolá During the California
Expedition of 1769–1770", ed. by D. E. Smith and F. J. Teggart, *in* Acad. of Pac. Coast
Hist., *Publications*, Vol. 1, No. 3 (1909), entry for 5 November, *before* Ortega made a
further exploration to the *contra costa*. [hereinafter, Portolá *Diary*].

Zoeth Skinner Eldredge, *The Beginnings of San Francisco* (1912), I, pp. 24–35, pro-
vides an account, quite speculative, about Ortega's exploration, which tells us that
Ortega reached Pt. Lobos, mounted the mesa back of Fort Point, and then climbed
Telegraph Hill for a full view of the Bay.

[25] This report about visibility conditions must refer to the immediate coastal area
and to the conditions within the Bay itself, because we note in the 31 October entry of
Costansó's *Diary* that there had been an argument the "day before" about whether Pt.
Reyes was a point of land or an island because there was mist in the vicinity of the
point.

of November sighting by Ortega can be deemed the more possible through the known facts of good visibility than if these facts were not known. It is difficult to imagine that trained scouts, and in the realm of scouting and trail-breaking Ortega, the leader of the party, was one of the greatest ever to appear on the American scene, could have moved with "tunnel vision" down the peninsula and have thus failed quite early in their march to have seen the southern arm of the Bay.

Did the Ortega party reach the Golden Gate or see the Golden Gate? There is convincing proof that they saw enough of the indentation of the coast-line to realize that the sea would join with the "estuary"; that this estuary was, indeed, "an arm of the sea". However, there are many reasons which may lead one to believe that the explorers did not reach the Gate or that they even advanced to places from which the Gate can actually be seen.[26]

---

[26] Professor Bolton was completely convinced that Sergeant Ortega had sighted the Golden Gate. In relating the return of Ortega to the San Pedro Camp Bolton wrote: "Ortega returned a few hours behind the hunters [*sic*], with the news that his way to Point Reyes was cut off by a roadstead that led into the estuary described by the hunters—a noble harbor that was almost land-locked, so near together stood the two titanic pillars of its one gate, open to the sunset ocean." See Bolton, *Crespi*, pp. xxvi-xxvii.

Ortega actually returned to camp not a few hours behind the hunters but a full twenty-four hours later than they, and prior to his return, Costansó and the other members of the expedition had surmised from the hunters' reports about the estuary that Ortega would not have been able to get around that body of water and reach Pt. Reyes in the time allowed him. No such poetic reference as the one quoted above appears in any of the documents, though Ortega and Crespí later wrote about the inner port being surrounded by mountains [see quoted descriptions in text, p. 30 ff.]. Also Crespí wrote to Palóu, 6 February 1770, from San Diego, explaining that the inner port was probably better than the outer port and that *if its depth* were great enough [see text for quotation, p. 30] large ships might be able to enter. In the Bolton translation we find the expression "it would seem that its *mouth* would therefore be large", because the word *fondo*, for depth, is translated as *mouth*. This error in translation may have contributed to Bolton's belief that the members of the Portolá expedition had *seen* the *mouth*, or the acceptance of the idea that the mouth had been seen might have caused the error in translation. See in addition, notes 43 and 45, below.

Professor Bolton also wrote a separate footnote, *ibid.*, p. xxviii, in which he tackled head-on the "Gate question". The note states: "A good deal of debate has been indulged in as to whether Ortega saw the entrance to the harbor. Unquestionably he saw it, for the records of the Portolá expedition plainly tell us so. From camp at San Pedro Point he was sent north to explore, with Point Reyes as an objective. After going 'about three leagues' he reached the 'end or head of the estuary' which the hunters had described. There his way was blocked by a 'very noble and very large harbor' ... 'on the parallel of thirty-eight degrees.' There were 'three islands within the

In explaining where Ortega went, Father Crespí stated in his diary that " . . . from the place which they had reached, which was the end or head of the estuary . . . " (the Spanish words being

---

strait which connects with the ocean between some high mountains'—the pillars of the Golden Gate. On the basis of Ortega's reports of his visit to the Golden Gate and of his tour around to the Contra Costa, Costansó, engineer and map-maker, drafted a map of San Francisco Bay that was strikingly accurate, showing the passage to the ocean, and two arms of the bay, between the Point Richmond and Alviso of today."

Taking up the items in the footnote, it must be emphatically asserted that there is simply no statement in the documents to the effect that Ortega reached the end or head of the estuary after going three leagues to the north and that this was at thirty-eight degrees.

The "end or head of the estuary" statement is found in the Crespí diary of 1769 and, as already explained, is not self-defining [see text, pp. 23 ff.]. The "three leagues" and "thirty-eight" degrees are mentioned in the letter which Crespí wrote to Palóu, 6 February 1770, from San Diego. Therein Crespí stated that his measurement of 37° 49' [for the San Pedro Camp area] was 11 minutes short of 38°, and that he made this measurement some three leagues "this side of the port."

That Crespí's statement must be taken quite literally is corroborated by Father Verger's statement in 1772 when he explains that the 1769 expedition discovered the following: that *Punta de Almejas* [now San Pedro Point] had a latitude of 37° 35' and that *Punta de los Reyes* had a latitude of 37° 44', but that the latter figure was an esti-mate, since Pt. Reyes was not reached. [It should be noted that Father Verger was probably using the lower figures provided by Engineer Costansó, rather than those given by Crespí. Costansó's latitudes are included in a table in Ortega's letter to Palóu, 9 February 1770.]

In other words, whether the latitudes used are those provided by Crespí or by Costansó, the intent is the same; namely, to show the distance in minutes of latitude (equated with distance in leagues) to the presumed position of the "port", as related to the San Pedro Camp. The explorers sometimes provide specific examples of the equating of distance on land with their observations of latitude. [See below, this foot-note.] But the presumed position of the "port" was just under Point Reyes whose dis-tance had to be estimated. Thus, the three leagues statement in the Bolton footnote cannot be set into a context which would lead one to believe that Ortega had marched to the "port" within a distance of three leagues.

The statement in the footnote about the "very noble and very large harbor" and to the "three islands" refers to information which comes *later* in the reports, not *before* Ortega had made his exploration in the *contra costa*, and cannot, therefore, be related to the first exploration [see text, pp. 30, ff.].

Finally, with reference to the Costansó map, the first thing one must recognize is that all the early explorers were firm in their acceptance of Cabrera's description about an entrance into the land. The southern arm of the Bay was seen by Ortega, by the deer hunters, and by the entire Portolá expedition [the latter event, 4 November]. The northern arm of the Bay was seen from above present Hayward during Ortega's second exploration along the *contra costa*.

The Costansó map, which is in very small scale, appears to this writer to be a con-struction by the engineer based upon the Cabrera Bueno description, Costansó's own belief that he had seen the mouth of an estuary [p. 18, above], and the known existence of the two arms of the Bay. This view of the matter seems sustained by the appear-ance of the Bay in the map, since the entrance is drawn to be almost as wide as the

remate ó cabeza), they were supposedly two marches from the port with the ship in it. Unfortunately, these words are not self-defining; they do not explain which head or end is being referred to.

---

arms of the Bay. Yet all the explorers who in later years actually saw the "Gate" made their visual estimate to be less than a league.

Also on his map Costansó placed the entrance into the land at 37° 40', yet he measured the latitude at the San Pedro Camp, according to the table in the Ortega letter previously referred to, at 37° 35'. Had the actual distance from the San Pedro Camp, or even the approximate distance, to the "Gate" been known, it is unlikely that Costansó would have considered that entrance to be but five nautical miles north of the camp. That Costansó equated minutes of latitude to nautical miles may be noted in his diary for 14 November, when the party was again moving south [see Costansó, *Diary*, entry for that date where four minutes of latitude are taken as being equal to "quatro millas maritimas", which is, of course, correct, since the nautical mile is by definition equal to a minute of latitude].

The Costansó map includes the peculiar quirk that it places Cabrera Bueno's Port of San Francisco *north* of Pt. Reyes. This was a probable mis-reading by Costansó of that part of the Cabrera Bueno *derrota* where the port is described as being *north* of the headland *but* on its eastern side [italics, T.E.T.]. [See Appendix, Cabrera Bueno *Derrota*.]

When all is said and done about the "Gate question", it is possible that a specific reference to the sighting of the Golden Gate by Ortega may still be found, even though such a reference has not come to light despite the research of numerous investigators among whom Professor Bolton was pre-eminent. Were documentation of an Ortega sighting of the Gate to be discovered, it would still have to be admitted that proof of such discovery has not yet been offered in acceptable form by any investigator.

The nearest specific reference to a sighting of the "Gate" seen by this writer is found in Father Verger's statement, a part of which was used above, this footnote. The full statement in Spanish and in translation follows, with this writer's further comment:

"Hallase el nominado Puertto entre el cabo de Almejas su latitud es de 37 grados y 35 m. y la puntta de Reyes tiene de latitud 37 grados y 44 m. segun congetturaron; por no haver podido llegar a ell. En este interrmedio se halla una grande ensenada con los farallones que refieren las Historias. En medio de la qual habre la tierra cerca de una legua y por ella se interna el mar como 15 leguas por el sur sueste; formando un brajo o estero de quattro leguas de ancho en parttes; y en otras de tres de dos y a lo ultimo de una legua . . . "

The translation reads: "The port mentioned [Cabrera's "port of San Francisco"] is found between Cape de Almejas, latitude 37° 35', and Pt. Reyes, latitude 37° 44', according to conjecture because it was not reached. In between is found a great inlet with the farallones mentioned in the histories. In the middle the land opens for about a league and through it the sea enters for about 15 leagues to the south southeast; forming an arm or estuary which is four leagues wide in parts, and in others, three or two, and finally, one league . . . " [*AGI*, Aud. de Guad., 512, microfilm, Bancroft Library, Roll III, Chapman number 1939, Verger to Viceroy, Mexico, 25 December 1772].

This kind of quotation is enough to make an investigator shout for joy, since it seems to establish a knowledge of the "Golden Gate" as gained by the first expedition. However, a further reading shows that Father Verger throughout his "representation" combined information from the 1769 and 1772 Bay expeditions [see pp. 39 ff., text], and it is, therefore, not clear that the quoted statement refers only to the 1769 exploration.

When other writings are considered—those of Crespí, Costansó, and Fages—it is quite apparent that these words were used to describe the south end of the Bay, not the end at, or nearest, its mouth.

Later, in speaking of their camp site (6 to 11 November, in the Palo Alto area) Crespí says they were four or five leagues short of the end of the estuary (*4 ó 5 leguas antes del remate de este estero*),[27] and he also refers to the same camp site as being that distance from where the estuary could be headed, in the words "*como a quatro ó cinco (leguas) para acabar de descabezar el dho estero*".[28] In 1772, in describing the Bay, when he had seen not only its southern arm, but also the "Gate", and San Pablo Bay, Father Crespí wrote that the Bay ends in a point or head to the south-southeast (*Remata en la punta ó cabeza del Sursueste*) and that the Round Bay (San Pablo Bay) at its end (*remate*) turned toward the northeast, i.e., into the Carquinez Strait.[29]

As if to confuse the question still further, a form of Engineer Costansó's diary which has recently come to light uses a different expression from that written by Father Crespí when the latter reported where Ortega and his men had got to. Crespí stated they reached the end or head of the estuary, but Costansó says "the end or head of the ridge [*Serro*]."[30]

Thus, the evidence found in word-usage would lead one to guess that Ortega and his men followed the ridge past "Fog Gap" and in the course of their march, perhaps even at the same position, saw both the indentation of the coast and the southern arm of the Bay. With their understanding of what Cabrera Bueno had written, that the sea entered the land, and from seeing the coastal indentation and the estuary, the exploring party might have decided to move toward the estuary for the purpose of trying to get around it. In the realm of word-usage lies also the fact that only when Crespí and Costansó were describing the view of the outer Port of

---

[27] Crespí to Palóu, San Diego, 6 February 1770.

[28] *Ibid.*, to Father Andrés, San Diego, 8 February 1770.

[29] Both forms of the Crespí diary for 1772 (see note 62, below). See also the Costansó *Narrative*, and the Fages diaries of 1770 and 1772.

[30] Bolton Papers (C-B 840 Part 1), Alta California, Item #88, Folder #1, photocopy from Legajo #53, *Biblioteca Nacional*, Mexico.

San Francisco, when they had Cabrera Bueno's description in mind, did they speak of an estuary mouth, using the words *boca* and *bocana*. These words are never used after that until the "Gate" is being described by men who are actually standing where they could see it, which was not until November 1770, and thereafter.[31]

When we turn to an examination of what Ortega reported as something actually seen, we discover the following. The explorers stated that there were two islands within the estuary.[32] From Point Lobos one can look through the Golden Gate and see one island, namely, Angel Island. From Fort Point three islands are visible; Angel, Alcatraz, and Yerba Buena. However, Ortega did not report seeing *three* islands until after his return from his later expedition along the eastern shore of the Bay. Then he had reached a position from where the three islands named are visible, but, as is revealed in the Fages exploration of 1770, considerably south of the latitude from where one can see the Golden Gate.

The only eminence near the end of the peninsula from where one can see two islands, namely, Angel and Yerba Buena, is San Bruno Mountain, but from the top of that land-form a view of the Gate is blocked.[33] If the information about the two islands as stated in Portolá's diary is correct, the top of San Bruno Mountain might have been the place from where Ortega and his men had their best view of the Bay.

The explorers of this era were good trail-finders and good trail-blazers. If one party had preceded another, the later comers usually told about seeing the evidences of the earlier group. Therefore, when we learn that in December, 1774, Captain Rivera (who had been with the Portolá expedition) with Father Francisco Palóu explored near the Golden Gate; that they were at a position from where they could see the harbor mouth and one island; and that they were "where no Spaniard nor any Christian" had set foot, we know that they were speaking quite literally.[34] The same con-

---

[31] See the Fages exploration of 1770, pp. 35 ff., text.

[32] Portolá *Diary*, entry for 5 November, 1769.

[33] This can be confirmed by a visit to San Bruno Mountain; see also Rivera's description of what he saw from this eminence, p. 59, text.

[34] Palóu, 1774, *Diary*, 4 December entry; see pp. 60–61, text.

clusion may be drawn from Lt. Col. Anza's report which was
made after he had stood on the height of the Cantil Blanco (Fort
Point) in the year 1776, during his exploration for the location of
the presidio and mission sites; namely, that on 26 March he went
to the narrowest opening made by the mouth of the port, "where
nobody had been before."[35]

We should also notice that among the explorers who saw the
Golden Gate between 1770 and 1776 there existed a consensus in
their visual estimates of its width; that it is an extremely narrow
entrance. The estimate of greatest width was made by Father
Crespí in 1772 from the *contra costa*, that of about three-quarters of
a league. But Lieutenant Fages, earlier than Crespí, in 1770, also
seeing the mouth of the Bay from its eastern side, described its
width as about three hundred *varas*. Fages, who like Rivera had
been with the Portolá expedition, wrote about his sighting of the
entrance as though it were a discovery. Father Font, who was
with Anza, considered the entrance to the Bay so narrow that it
could be defended with muskets. Yet Sergeant Ortega described
the estuary as being not less than two leagues in width at its narrowest point. Would he have written thus had he seen the
"Gate"?[36]

Before Ortega and his party of explorers returned to the San
Pedro camp from wherever they had been, Costansó, Crespí, and
others, as noted, had already made the assumption, as a result of
the previous report of the deer hunters about a great estuary, that
Ortega could not have reached Point Reyes in the time that had
been allotted him. Commander Portolá now decided to continue
his exploration for a few days more, evidently with the hope of
finding a way around the water barrier to reach the port with the
ship in it.[37]

The 4th of November, 1769, in retrospect becomes the most
notable of all the days during this first exploration of the San

---

[35] Anza, *Diary*; see below, footnote 125.

[36] Crespí, *Diary*, 1772; Fages, *Diary*, 1770; and Font, see pp. 81–82, text. Ortega to
Palóu, 9 February 1770, San Diego, in Palóu, *Historical Memoirs*, IV, p. 287.

[37] This decision was not stated on 3 November, but becomes apparent in the program followed by the expedition in the next few days, and on the 7th when Sergeant
Ortega was sent out on his second exploration, this time of the *contra costa*.

Francisco Bay region, because one moment on that day marked the first time that the entire membership of the expedition, including its leader, Commander Portolá, saw the great sweep of the southern arm of San Francisco Bay. The day began auspiciously, for the members of the expedition recognized the 4th of November as the day of San Carlos, the patron of the presidio and mission which were to be established at Monterey, and also the patron of King Charles III. A solemn mass was celebrated. Father Crespí in describing this service states that without any doubt the place where they held it was "in the little valley at the beach of the Port of San Francisco." They left camp at one o'clock in the afternoon, following the shoreline for a short distance.

"We soon entered the sierra," wrote Costansó, "following to the northeast, and on the summit of a ridge [doubtless Sweeney Ridge][38] we descried a grand estuary which extended to the southeast and south-southeast. Keeping it to our left, and turning our back to the *Puerto* [i.e., the outer Port of San Francisco], we followed a canyon which opened to the south and southeast, and

---

[38] Dr. F. M. Stanger, San Mateo County historian, has stated that on September 29, 1947, "Dr. Bolton in person attended a meeting, at this spot [i.e., Sweeney Ridge], of the San Francisco Portolá Festival Committee, together with leading members of the San Mateo County Historical Association. He accepted there our findings and sanctioned the dedication of this spot as the site of the discovery of San Francisco Bay."

The most convincing evidence to this writer in favor of the Sweeney Ridge site is found in the topography of the region and in the compass "fix" obligingly provided by Costansó in his 1 November entry where he states that the position of Pt. Reyes from the San Pedro Camp was west, 16 degrees northwest. If one swings around to a NE line from the Pt. Reyes fix, which would be 119 degrees, the direction indicated is directly toward the hills. The topography of the region then dictates a march toward Sweeney Ridge.

The Sweeney Ridge site has been registered as a California State Landmark. Recently, Dr. Stanger, Mrs. R. L. Spangler, President of the Portolá Expedition Bicentennial Foundation, and their associates, have developed a program which has as its purpose the gaining of National Historic Landmark recognition for the Sweeney Ridge site. [This national recognition was granted on 17 May 1968 by Secretary of the Interior Stewart Udall.] The site would then become a park as a feature of a proposed Skyline Parkway and the dedication of the site, hopefully, would occur in November 1969, the two-hundred anniversary of the Portolá march, and on the precise day of November 4, when the entire Portolá expedition had its first sight of San Francisco Bay.

The present writer has been in support of the objectives of the Portolá Expedition Bicentennial Foundation and accepts the Sweeney Ridge site and the 4 November date as symbolic in place and in time of the discovery, although the record clearly shows that the southern arm of the Bay had been seen earlier by some members of the expedition.

at the setting of the sun camped in the shelter of the oaks which bordered the foothill of the ridges on the west."[39]

After the journey of the 4th of November, during which the party had traveled only two leagues, two additional marches were made so that by the 6th of November camp had been made in the general vicinity of San Francisquito Creek in the present Palo Alto area. During the 6th of November a strenuous effort was made through sign language to learn from the numerous natives where the port with the ship in it might be—Costansó stated that the men asked *mil preguntas* of the natives—but they were unable to arrive at any conclusion except that there was no real communication possible.[40]

---

[39] Costansó, especially in his form of the diary in Legajo 53, makes clear what is meant by the *south shore or beach* of the San Pedro Camp; namely, that it was understood by all to be the south shore of Cabrera's Port of San Francisco. Dr. Bolton must have been convinced that Crespí had made an error in providing directions in his entry for 4 November. Crespí wrote: " . . . á la una de la tarde salimos para proseguir el viaje, siguiendo la playa del *Sur* . . . " [italics, T.E.T.]. This Bolton rendered as: "About one in the afternoon we set out to continue the journey, following the beach *to the north*" [italics, T.E.T.]. The translation should read: " . . . following the *south* beach [i.e., of Cabrera's Port of San Francisco]." In justification of Professor Bolton's translation it should be said that he understood how the party, following beach, would *not* have proceeded *south* but must have followed the beach toward the north before ascending the hills where the estuary was then seen by them. Therefore, his presentation of where the explorers went is correct, but the geographical basis for his conclusion did not include an understanding of the "south beach" concept.

After the explorers had viewed the southern arm of the Bay from atop Sweeney Ridge, Crespí and Costansó (according to both Teggart and Bolton) stated: "Keeping it [the estuary] always on the left hand, and, turning our backs to the bay, we took a valley open to the south, etc."

This statement becomes intelligible only when it is given as: "Keeping it [the estuary] always on the left hand, and, turning our backs to the Port [of Cabrera Bueno], we took a valley open to the south, etc."

Finally, in the same passage, Dr. Bolton points out that after leaving the ridge the explorers went toward the south and southwest and that "all the texts" are in agreement that the direction followed was south and southwest. [Bolton, *Crespi*, p. 231, note #115]. It is true that the Palôu-Figueroa text states "sur sureste", but both forms of the Costansó diary [note 19, above] clearly state that the direction was to the southeast [*sursueste*]. The Costansó forms are being followed here as being in consonance with the topography which both Crespí and Costansó were describing.

Father Crespí and Engineer Costansó both wrote with some admiration about the view they had of the great estuary or arm of the sea when they first saw it from Sweeney Ridge on the 4th of November. Commander Portolá, however, was in a sour mood on that day. His *Diary* states, simply: "We traveled for three hours; the entire road was bad. We halted without water." Later, Portolá expressed appreciation of the Bay and of its suitability as a site for a mission and a presidio [see p. 33, text].

[40] Legajo 53.

Therefore, on the 7th of November, Ortega and the scouts were again sent out, this time on a four-day mission—presumably because the port with the ship in it lay at a distance of a journey of two days from some point that Ortega had reached on his first exploration from the San Pedro Camp—and natives were taken along as guides.[41] The exploring party returned to camp on the evening of the 10th, and this time no musket shots, harbingers of good news, announced their return. Their mood was one of dejection. They were now persuaded that Monterey lay behind them; they had found no indications of the proximity of the Port; they had seen another immense estuary lying to the northeast, which extended far into the land and joined with the one extending to the southeast; they believed it would take them as much time to get around this second estuary as it had taken to get around the first one. Furthermore, the natives in the *contra costa* had not been friendly, and had been completely unintelligible in their sign language.

Commander Portolá's evaluation of the second Ortega exploration was expressed in his usual laconic style. "All the time they were gone," he wrote of the explorers, "they skirted the shore of this arm of the sea or port; they returned after four days and reported that they had found nothing, leaving us in doubt as to whether we could find anything farther on."[42] A Council of War was held on the 11th of November and it was agreed that the party would retrace its steps and attempt again to find the Port of Monterey.

The discovery of San Francisco Bay was without question the major achievement of the Portolá expedition of 1769, and also of

[41] Portolá *Diary* states that Captain Fernando de Rivera commanded the sergeant [Ortega] and eight soldiers to go out and explore.

[42] Costansó states that the council meeting was held on the morning of the 11th of November. Portolá included reference to the council meeting in an entry headed with the date, 7 November. That entry, however, turns out to be a composite one, summarizing events from the 7th to the 11th. Portolá in this entry described the failure of the scouts to find "any of the indications of the Port of Monterey as given by Cabrera Bueno" and that the expedition "turned back on the 11th of November."

The diaries of Costansó, Crespí, and Portolá mention estuary [singular] prior to the *contra costa* exploration. The Costansó *Narrative* [note 20, above], a "smooth" version, written later, uses the plural, *estuaries*, as does Ortega in his letter to Palóu from San Diego. In the latter two cases the descriptions are summaries, based upon *both* of Ortega's explorations. The northern arm of the Bay was not referred to until Ortega had made his second, or *contra costa*, exploration from the Palo Alto camp.

the entire era of early Spanish exploration in Alta California. Even
though Portolá eventually succeeded in finding Monterey Bay,
which had been his original purpose, the grandeur of the great inland Bay was ultimately recognized by all, including especially
officials in the highest echelon of the Spanish administrative
hierarchy. Thus, the later decision to establish a presidio and two
missions in the environs of the Bay came as a result of the realization that the Bay was there and that it was a superb port.

It is essential, then, to give some consideration to the writings
of the first explorers in their descriptions of what they had found.
Quite apparently Crespí, Ortega, Rivera, and Portolá, whose
writings will be examined, not only described what they saw but
also almost at once began to express value judgments about the
advantages of the great inland body of water. The most prolix of
the four, as befitted a man of letters, was Father Juan Crespí.

"This Port of San Francisco," wrote he, "as we saw, and in the
understanding of all those intelligent [ones of the expedition], is
very large, and without doubt the port in which are the farallones
could [contain] not only all the armadas of our Catholic Monarch
but also all those of Europe.[43]

"This most grand estuary or arm of the sea, has its entrance between high mountains, and they say that within it [the estuary]
appear three islands, which we were not able to see where we were
because of being too low.[44] This estuary is surrounded on all sides
by high mountains throughout its entire length, so that it becomes a
lake, as it were, protected from all the winds.

"Now considering that this most noble estuary is three leagues
wide at the narrowest place throughout its whole extent, it would
seem that its depth would therefore be great and that ships could

---

[43] The description here is from the letter which Crespí wrote to the Franciscan
Guardian, Father Juan Andrés, on 8 February 1770, dated at San Diego. It must be
considered with the letter which Professor Bolton translated and included in the
Crespi volume, the one of 6 February 1770, San Diego, addressed to Father Francisco
Palóu. The letter to Palóu does *not* explain that Crespí looked upon the Port of San
Francisco as consisting in the combined *outer* [present Gulf of the Farallones] and *inner*
ports, and his reference to the size of the port in the Palóu letter leaves the impression
that he is writing only about the inner body of water when he is, as a matter of fact,
writing about the combined bays.

[44] Treutlein translation.

enter even though they were of [great size *or* of deep draught—*alto bordo*—], and I do not doubt that in time it will be possible to sound it and to explore it.[45]

"The idea that we have formed of this large and most noble Port of Our Father San Francisco is that there are two such, one outer in which are the six or seven farallones as Cabrera says, and the other, better one, shielded from all winds, within the said estuary or arm of the sea. Therefore if after a time the ships do not find the Port of Monterey, which I doubt completely [they can], since so many eyes searched for it, and with such care because finding it was our entire obligation, we have in place of it this so very excellent [Port] of San Francisco in which to set up the standard of the Holy Cross and from which to convert to our holy Catholic Faith the numerous friendly and kindly Indians who inhabit the land round about this estuary."[46]

And the man who had up to that time seen more of the Bay than anyone except his fellow scouts, Sergeant Ortega, wrote to Father Palóu that the estuary was "an excellent port." He estimated the length of the southern arm of the Bay as more than eighteen leagues and said that its width varied from two to four leagues. What particularly impressed Ortega was the security of the Port. "And within, the shelter is so great between the mountains it is

---

[45] Treutlein translation. The key word in this passage is *fondo*, which has to do with depth, with the *bottom* of a body of water. In short, Crespí says nothing whatever about the *mouth* or *entrance* of the Bay. The Spanish for the quoted passage reads: " . . . parese que desde luego su *fondo* será grande, y que en el pudieran entrar Navios mas que fueran de alto bordo, etc." [italics, T.E.T.]. This was translated by Dr. Bolton: " . . . it would seem that its *mouth* would therefore be large and that ships could enter even though they were of deep draught, etc." [italics, T.E.T.].

In the documents the words *boca* or *bocana*, for mouth or entrance are used on 30 October 1769 when the members of the Portolá expedition thought they were viewing the entrance into the land of Cabrera Bueno's estuary [see, p. 17, text]. After that they are never used until reference is being made to a visual sighting of the "Gate". Had the mouth been sighted at the time Crespí wrote, no question would have been raised about the size of the mouth relative to the size of a ship; however, its width might have been mentioned (as was always done on later occasions during visual sighting), and its depth questioned [see Fages expedition, 1770, pp. 35 f., text].

[46] Crespí also wrote to the Visitor-General, Joseph de Gálvez, where his description of the "estuary" was given as "a very great and magnificent port, with shelter from all winds" and he referred to the Indians dwelling upon its shores in their many and large villages as "affable, mild, docile and generous heathen." Crespí to Gálvez, 9 February 1770, San Diego, in Bolton, *Crespí.*

like unto a securely locked chest, which made me realize that my master would have no other like it, if its depth is in proportion [to its size and shape]."[47]

Ortega's concluding paragraph indicates how greatly all members of the exploring party were impressed by the grandeur of the Bay: "Finally, on the 11th of November we left this estuary in accordance with a conference that was held in regard to it and as necessity demanded, although if we had had provisions I think that we would have settled there and would have informed the superiors, since there was a harbor, good land, wood and countless Indians, although it is rather far north." To which may be added that Captain Rivera, writing succinctly as he usually did, stated in a report to Viceroy Croix that if the port had adequate depth its several advantages would make it preferable to San Diego, since its environs had "firewood, abundant timber, running water, good lands, and people."[48]

When the expedition had returned to San Diego, Captain Portolá penned a report to the Viceroy to explain his failure to reach Monterey. It must be recognized that this report is after the fact and may thus be considered a rationalization. He stated that when the expedition had turned back they first decided to wait at the Santa Barbara channel because "that is a better supplied country" and if then a vessel had reached them they "might again undertake the expedition, if not to Monterrey, then to the Port of San Francisco . . . " However, they did have to return to San Diego "where the whole expedition now is, without even a single man having been lost."[49]

---

[47] Ortega to Palóu, San Diego, February 9, 1770 in Palóu, *op. cit.*, pp. 286–291. The Spanish for the Ortega quotation is: " . . . y adentro abrigo grandissimo entre sierra y sierra de manera, que es una Caja Cerrada con muchas llaves, que me hizo conozer, que mi amo no tendrá otro semejante, si el fondo es correspondiente." The Bolton translation for this is: " . . . and within there is a very large harbor between mountains, of such a sort that it is like a box locked by many keys, which made me recognize the fact that if the depth is in proportion my master has no other like it."

[48] Transcript, Bolton Papers, Item #90, Folder #27, Alta California, 2 March 1770, Rivera to Croix, written at Velicatá, Baja California. [See note 62, below, for reference to the Bolton Papers].

[49] This letter, dated 11 February 1770 at San Diego, was published in the Magazine Section, Part I, October 17, 1909, *The San Francisco Sunday Call*. Dr. H. E. Bolton, who found and translated the letter, was at that time Professor of History at Stanford University. Copy in Bolton Papers, Item #90, Folder #26, Alta California.

In this same letter Captain Portolá also revealed that his own Diary of the expedition had not yet been completed because he had been so extremely busy, but that he would attend to this matter as soon as he could. "Lack of it [the Diary] may be supplied at present by the one which I believe is being sent by Don Miguel Costansó to His Illustriousness" (namely, Joseph de Gálvez).[50]

The foregoing information was dated 11 February 1770, and a second letter, 17 April 1770, then outlined to the Viceroy how Portolá still hoped to carry out his orders for establishing a presidio and a mission in the north. During the interval between the dates the *San Antonio* (*El Príncipe*) under Captain Juan Pérez had reached San Diego, a circumstance which may have saved the entire venture.[51]

Portolá then arranged that Pérez would sail north and reconnoiter the Port of San Francisco, i.e., Cabrera's bay; he would then drop down "until he finds a large estuary which extends into the land twelve or sixteen leagues, which it appeared to all of us might very well be a port, and at the same time a place very well suited to the establishment of a mission, and which Don Miguel Costansó, who is to embark, knows very well"; and that then Pérez would descend to Monterey which he, Portolá, hoped the seamen would find, although the land expedition had not.

Thus, reasoned Portolá, if Monterey existed, both expeditions (his land party, and the *San Antonio*) would have the good fortune to find themselves at their destination, "but if it [Monterey] should not exist, or rather, if it should be at the Port of San Francisco, or at the other place cited [that is, modern San Francisco Bay], that the Mission and Presidio should be established."

But the good soldier Portolá assured the Viceroy that "under all circumstances I shall *always* give preference to the Port of

The year 1909 was the one hundred and fortieth anniversary of the arrival of the Portolá expedition. The California Promotion Committee in that year brought out Z. S. Eldredge's *The March of Portolá*.

[50] Bolton Papers, *ibid*.

[51] *Ibid*., Folder #31. See Geiger, *Serra*, I, Ch. XXX, "The Fate of San Diego Hangs in the Balance" for an excellent and thoroughly documented discussion of the near-disaster of the entire northern [Upper] California enterprise. This chapter is distinguished for its balanced presentation and should be read as a corrective to the romanticized sectarianism which has surrounded the San Diego crisis.

Monterrey in order not to depart a jot from my blind and resigned obedience."[52]

The words of Ortega and Portolá and Rivera's brief praise, taken together in their meaning and in their chronological relationship, all pertaining to the "estuary", raise the fascinating possibility that mere accident or circumstance prevented the founding of a mission and a presidio on the shores of the present San Francisco Bay in 1769, and perhaps again in 1770.[53] In the former instance, it was apparently lack of supplies which prevented that action; in the latter case, Captain Juan Pérez did not find the "Golden Gate" and therefore failed also to find the "large estuary which extends into the land". However, Pérez did reach Monterey Bay, as did Portolá. So Portolá's promise to the Viceroy that he would *always* give preference to the Port of Monterey could be kept, and the Royal Presidio of Monterey and Mission San Carlos were founded on 3 June 1770.

For the time being, when the *Official Account* of the Portolá expedition was printed, which told of the ultimate triumph at Monterey, nothing was said about the exploration of the great estuary.[54] The reasons for this omission are several. The expedition had accomplished its original purpose and this accomplishment had to be emphasized. Moreover, it took some time for the highest administrative officials, not to mention the men who were actually in the field as explorers, to adjust their geographical understanding to what was not yet to them a new discovery. It required about four years of additional exploration and further thinking to separate the concept of a hitherto unknown inland estuary from Cabrera Bueno's description of the bay or port under Point Reyes which also had an inner estuary, friendly natives, and good water.

---

[52] Bolton Papers, Item #90, Folder #31.

[53] The chronology of these letters may be summarized as follows:

    9 Feb. 1770, San Diego, Ortega to Palóu.

    11 Feb. 1770, San Diego, Portolá to Viceroy.

    2 Mar. 1770, Velicatá, Baja California, Rivera to Viceroy.

    17 Apr. 1770, San Diego, Portolá to Viceroy.

[54] Translated as "The Official Account of the Portolá Expedition of 1769–1770" *in* Acad. of Pac. Coast Hist., *Publications*, Vol. 1, No. 2 (1909). The original was published in Mexico, 16 August 1770.

4

The First Fages Exploration: 1770

Efforts to resolve the geographical confusion about the bays, ports, and estuaries now known to exist north of Monterey led to a whole series of new explorations. The first of these was unofficial and provides a good example of the individual initiative which was possible within the framework of the authoritarian system of Spanish administration. Lieutenant of Volunteers of Cataluña, Don Pedro Fages, had succeeded Don Gaspar de Portolá as military commander of Upper California, after the latter's departure following the founding of the presidio and mission at Monterey.

Fages now decided to do what the Ortega exploration had failed to accomplish; namely, to find a land route to the "Port of San Francisco." With six soldiers and one muleteer, Fages left Monterey on November 17, 1770, and proceeded northwestward until they reached the Santa Clara Valley. This Fages named *La Cañada del Puerto de San Francisco*. Following down the valley they made camp on the 26th of November in a locality which Fages described as the head of the estuary of the Port of San Francisco (*en la cabesa del estero del Puerto de San Francisco*).

From this camp the party moved along the east shore of the estuary and "succeeded in going about seven leagues beyond the place where the explorers of the expedition of the previous year [Ortega and his eight men] were. From the top of a hill at this place", wrote he, "there was seen a large estuary mouth [*bocana*], which, as it appeared to me and to the soldiers, was about three hundred *varas* wide, and reached about the same distance inland and another a little narrower. Through these [mouths] ran a great quantity of water from the sea, forming two large estuaries. The one which we had at our left must have turned south about fifteen leagues, and of the other we saw some twenty leagues which ran toward the east. From all this we inferred that it was the estuary of the Port of San Francisco of which the itinerary of Cabrera Bueno speaks. Of it we could not see the end, which made it necessary for us to turn back, for it lay across our path. . . . "[55]

The sighting of the entrance to the Bay occurred on 28 Novem-

---

[55] "Expedition to San Francisco Bay in 1770. Diary of Pedro Fages," ed. by Herbert E. Bolton *in ibid.*, Vol. 2, No. 3 (1911). Up to the date of the publication of this diary it had been assumed that the Fages-Crespí expedition to the Bay in 1772 was the next one to follow the Portolá expedition of 1769. For instance, Davidson, *op. cit.*, p. 137, says, flatly: "The first name of the gate was given by Comandante Pedro Fagés [*sic*] on the 26th of March, 1772, when he looked through it from the Berkeley hills and named it 'La Bocana de la Enseñada [*sic*] de los Farallones.'"
We now know from the Bolton edition of the *first* Fages expedition that Fages and his men sighted the Bay entrance on 28 November 1770, and called the large mouth of the estuary *quantiosa vocana de estero*. Davidson's date for the sighting is not correctly given for the second Fages expedition and, since he had not used the 1770 diary which Bolton later discovered, his date for a *first* sighting is also incorrect. What is more difficult to understand than an error in a date is Davidson's implication that the entrance to the Bay was given a name. No proper name was given to the mouth of the Bay during either the Spanish or the Mexican era. The various forms for the entrance used in the 1772 Crespí diaries used by Davidson are: "la boca", "la Bocana", "la bocana del estero", and "la grande boca del Estero de Sn. Francisco paralelo a la ensenada de la punta de Reyes" [for reference to the Crespí diaries see pp. 39 ff., text, and note 62. The "newly discovered" Fages diary of 1772 is also referred to in note 62. For the microfilm of the 1770 Fages diary; Bancroft Library, *AGN*, Californias, Tomos 66, 67.
In the opinion of this writer it is incorrect to refer to the entrance of the Bay as the *Gate* if this term is used as part of a quoted translation from an Eighteenth Century document, for such usage unintentionally creates the impression that the word is a *name*, and that this name now used for the harbor entrance has a greater antiquity in its usage than is actually the case.
However, Brown's translation of Rivera's entry for 27 November is correct where the Spanish word *Puerta* is rendered *gateway* (see below, page 57). *Puerta* could also be rendered *gate*, but not *Gate*.
The "Golden Gate" was not so named until 1848, when this expression is found in the "Geographical Memoir" presented to the Senate of the United States by John Charles Frémont, in June of that year [Senate. Miscellaneous. No. 148. 30th Congress, 1st Session. June, 1848, Pages 44, and 23 pages of Appendix, with "Map of Oregon and Upper California from the surveys of John Charles Frémont and other authorities"].
In a footnote to page 32 Frémont adds: "Passing through this gate called Chrysopylae (Golden gate) on the map, on the same principle that the harbor of Byzantium (Constantinople afterwards) was called Chrysoceras (golden horn). The form of the harbor, and its advantages for commerce (and that before it became an entrepot of eastern commerce) suggested the name to the Greek founders of Byzantium. The form of the entrance into the Bay of San Francisco, and its advantages for commerce (Asiatic inclusive), suggest the name which is given to this entrance" [quoted from George Davidson, *The Discovery of San Francisco Bay* (1907), p. 138].

ber 1770 and this date is probably the correct discovery date for the Golden Gate, the *large mouth of the estuary (quantiosa vocana del estero)*. It should be remembered that Fages had been with the Portolá expedition. Clearly, he considered what he and his men saw as a discovery.

On November 29 Fages wrote: "This day, seeing that we were unable to cross to the other side—that of the Punta de los Reyes— without spending many days, and because of the anxiety which I felt for the camp, the cultivation of the land, and the raising of the stock, it was decided to go back . . . " And Fages concluded his brief diary, upon his arrival in Monterey, with the words: "This expedition was made in the service of His Majesty, with the object of reconnoitering the country as far as the Port of San Francisco."[56]

Lieutenant Fages had returned to Monterey on 4 December 1770 from his unsuccessful expedition. Meanwhile, Viceroy Croix in Mexico was preparing an order which would cause Fages again to proceed with the hope of attaining the same goal, that of finding a

---

[56] The quotations in the text are from Fages' diary and from a letter of transmittal prepared by Fages to accompany the diary. An endorsement on the back of the letter reads: "Monterey, June 20, 1771. Don Pedro Fages. Enclosing the diagram of that presidio, and reporting the discovery of two estuaries, one about fifteen and the other twenty leagues long." In view of the fact that the entire Portolá expedition had seen the southern arm of the Bay and that Ortega had explored part of it and had viewed a patch of San Pablo Bay, the endorsement seems only partly correct.

Crespí's evaluation of the expedition is noted in the text, p. 40. Fages himself stated his opinion of the major achievement of the 1770 expedition. He had, he said, discovered a road to the Bay which was ten leagues shorter and also better than when he made the journey from Monterey to the shores of the Bay with Portolá in 1769. See *Annales des voyages, de la geographie, de l'histoire et de l'archeologie,* "Voyage en Californie, Par D. Pedro Fages". (Translated from the Ms. inedited, in the M. Ternaux-Compans. Library, Vol. 101, where we see: " . . . en 1769, nous dépassâmes le port de Monterey et nous allâmes jusqu'aux lagunes de San-Francisco, qui sont situées trente-six lieues plus loin. Nous éprouvâmes de grandes difficultés à faire cette longue route comme à tâtons à travers un pays inconnu; mais lors de la seconde expédition, je partis avec quatre soldats et je parvins à découvrir une route que était non-seulement plus facile, mais de dix lieues plus courte.")

If one refers to the Costansó diary and adds up the "mileage" covered from Blancos near the shore of Monterey Bay where the Portolá expedition was encamped between the 2 and 6 of October, 1769, to the San Francisquito camp (circa Palo Alto) where they camped on 6 November, the distance equals 36 leagues. Crespí's distance is slightly greater. Thus, the statement by Fages that he had cut 10 leagues from the Monterey presidio to the south end of the Bay is quite accurate in his terms. Actually there were *seis,* not *quatre,* soldiers with Fages, but he might have had in mind the events of 28 November 1770, when four members of his party went out from the camp and reported seeing the mouth of the harbor.

way around the great "estuaries." The Viceregal order was dated
12 November 1770, and it reached Monterey on the 21st of May
1771. The Viceroy commanded that as soon as possible Fages
would "in accord with the Father President Junípero Serra" reconnoiter by land or by sea the Port of San Francisco so as to establish there a mission to the end that such an important place be not
exposed to foreign occupation. Viceroy Croix's sense of urgency
comes out strongly in his last sentence when he orders that
the San Francisco mission (as well as others previously referred
to in this same despatch) be established quickly as an object of
first attention.[57]

The Viceroy's action was the continuation of the impulse for
expansion and occupation provided by Visitor Gálvez and agreed
to by himself. The desire for haste apparent in his despatch was
reminiscent of the feelings expressed in orders previously written
about the need for planting settlements at Monterey. But the men
who were giving orders were still using the old language about
the "Port of San Francisco", and it would be some time before a
full realization would dawn upon them of the potentiality of the
"new Bay of San Francisco."[58]

Because of a change in administration the expansionist program
which had been developed by Gálvez and Viceroy Croix would be
continued, if that became his choice, by the new Viceroy, Antonio
María Bucareli y Ursúa, who assumed office in September, 1771.
Visitor Gálvez remained in New Spain until February, 1772 to
assist in orienting Bucareli. The Viceroy reported that he held
daily conferences with the Visitor for *four months*, and that he had
read a monumental report prepared by Gálvez, with "many
documents attached", and concluded that he "could not soon give a
solid opinion on the state of the viceroyalty in all parts. It must
await investigation, experience, and some handling of affairs",
concluded the cautious Bucareli.[59]

---

[57] In *Calif. Archives, Provincial State Papers*, Ms., I, 70, Bancroft Library.

[58] See above, text p. 10.

[59] Quotations from the excellent biography of Bucareli by Bobb, p. 31; see note #74,
below.

5

The Fages–Crespí Exploration of 1772 and the 1773 Decision to Strengthen Upper California

The second Fages expedition, initiated by Viceroy Croix, finally got started in March, 1772, almost a full year after Fages had received his orders to make it. Fages' own diary states simply that it was kept during the search being made for the Port of San Francisco.[60] Father Crespí, however, wrote a "Reason for the Undertaking" which provides the present-day reader with an excellent sense of the setting for the expedition of 1772.[61]

"The famous Port of San Francisco named in the navigation route of Admiral Cabrera Bueno and in the expedition of General Don Sebastian Vizcayno as intermediate between [the Port of] Monterey and Cape Mendocino, was seen confusedly by those who went on the expedition of the year 1769 when we were seeking [the Port of] Monterey," wrote Crespí. "As soon as we saw the farallones which indicate it and Point Reyes which incloses it in the inlet it forms with Cape de las Almejas, from this place the expedition turned back, assured now from the signs that Monterey lay behind. The year following, in the month of November, the mission and Royal Presidio of Monterey being established, an at-

---

[60] See note #62, below, for the citation for the Fages diary of 1772.

[61] *Ibid.*, below, for reference to the Sevilla Ms from which Crespí's "Reason for the Undertaking" is quoted. The form of the translation here is substantially that provided by Professor Bolton in *Crespi*, pp. 277–278, with certain changes preferred by this writer.

tempt was made by Lieutenant of Volunteers Don Pedro Fages (now Captain), Commandant of the said Royal Presidio, with an adequate number of soldiers, to go and see and examine the said Port, but there was little or almost nothing he could add to the first reports. That which was gained was that he discovered a straighter road, level and easy.

"Later there arrived the vessel, *El Príncipe*, in the month of May, bringing ten religious from the Apostolic College of San Fernando for the founding of five missions in this vast heathendom, and among these [missions] was named that of Our Seraphic Father San Francisco in his Port, the excellent Señor Viceroy ordering first an examination made by sea or by land, so as to carry out the said foundation, and with the occupation of that important Port for the Crown of Spain. The ship was not able to go at that time because of reasons given by its captain. For the landsmen neither was it possible to go because the founding of other missions was urgent, and the said Commandant went to San Diego to bring persons and mules for those foundations. Meanwhile, the Reverend Father President went with what he had to found Mission San Antonio de Padua, in the Valley of the Oaks, about twenty-five leagues distant from this one of Monterey. These things finished, and the heavy rains over, it now seemed necessary to undertake this expedition to take care of the foundation ordered as quickly as possible."

Captain Pedro Fages was accompanied by Father Crespí, six leather-jacket soldiers (*soldados de cuera*), a muleteer, and an Indian servant. Again Fages failed to reach his goal, Cabrera's "Port of San Francisco", but the explorers discovered the Carquinez Strait and the streams emptying into Suisun Bay from the Sacramento-San Joaquin systems. To the combined streams Father Crespí gave the name, *El Rio Grande de Nuestro Serafico Padre San Francisco*, and it was the opinion of some members of the expedition who had seen the Ebro River in Spain that the Ebro was not half as large as this new *Rio Grande*.

Then it was, on the 30th of March 1772, that Father Crespí ventured the opinion: "From all that we have seen and learned it is inferred that if the new mission must be established on the very

Port of San Francisco or in its vicinity, neither provisions nor stock can be taken to it by land; nor if it is founded will it be able to maintain any connection with this port of Monterey unless several canoes and some sailors are provided with which to go from one place to the other, to transport the necessities, and in this way make communication easy. May God our Lord, who penetrates hearts, show the rulers what to decide in order that they may make the decision most conducive to His greater honor and glory, and to the welfare of those helpless, blind, and unhappy souls. Amen".[62]

---

[62] Bolton, *Crespi*, pp. xxxix–xl. Professor Bolton used the Palóu-Figueroa Ms and the Spanish printed version in the Palóu *Noticias* to prepare his translation of the Crespí diary of 1772, but to it added the "Reason for the Undertaking" from the "original official draft of the diary", the so-called Sevilla Ms. In the "Reason" Crespí expressed his hope for a greater appreciation on the part of the "rulers" for the inner estuary. It should be noted that Crespí placed a different emphasis on the origin of the undertaking than did Palóu, *Historical Memoirs*, II, p. 328. Palóu wrote that " . . . the father president [Serra] decided that . . . Crespí should go and examine the harbor, for which purpose he also invited the captain commander Don Pedro Fages . . . " Crespí, however, says: " . . . the most excellent viceroy ordered that first an exploration should be made by land or sea to effect this foundation [on Cabrera's 'Port of San Francisco']." The interest on Serra's part in the expedition need not be minimized [see p. 44, text, and ff., for references to Serra's attitudes], but the 1772 expedition was clearly the result of the Viceroy's order.

The Sevilla Ms may be examined in microfilm, AGI, Aud. de Guad. 515, Roll II. The writer has used the above sources with the exception of the Figueroa Ms, and in addition has utilized what shall be called the Crespí-Verger form (Aud. de Guad., 512, Roll III), as well as a "newly discovered" diary kept by Pedro Fages himself. This latter diary thus brings to four the direct sources available for the 1772 Fages-Crespí expedition. Interesting aspects of the "re-discovery" of the diary of Captain Pedro Fages are discussed under the heading:

"The Case of the Missing Diary"

"The diary which was kept from the Mission and Royal Presidio of the Señor San Carlos of the Port of Monte-Rey in search of the Port of San Francisco. The corps of the Expedition was composed of the Reverend Father Fray Juan Chrespy, Captain Don Pedro Fages, fourteen soldiers, and a Christian Indian, a page to the Reverend Father."

[Diario que se hiso, desde la Mission y R.¹ Presidio del S.ᵒʳ S.ⁿ Carlos del Puerto de Monte=Rey; en busca del Puerto de S.ⁿ Franc.ᶜᵒ, y se compuso el Cuerpo de Esta Expedision del R.P.F. Juan Chrespy Cap.ⁿ D.ⁿ Pedro Fages catorze Soldados, y un Yndio Christiano Paje del R.P. Microfilm, Bancroft Library, *AGN*, Californias, 66, Reel 55].

The first printed reference to the 1772 Fages diary appeared in 1911, in the Academy of Pacific Coast History *Publications*, Vol. 2, No. 3 (Berkeley) when Dr. H. E. Bolton brought out the Spanish text with its translation of the Fages *Diary* of 1770 which he had recently discovered in Mexico. Until 1911 it was believed that the 1772 journey from Monterey to the Bay region had been the first such trip after the initial

Knowledge gained of the environs of the Bay resulted in the
preparation of a map which, though distorted, revealed many details of the Bay's geography unknown to Costansó who had pre-

---

Portolá discovery in 1769. Now, stated Bolton in his Introduction to the 1770 diary:
"It seems strange that, in *their* diaries of the expedition of 1772, over much the same
ground as that traversed in 1770, neither Crespi nor Fages mentions the earlier journey" [italics, T.E.T.]. Dr. Bolton's statement needed modification later when the
Crespí Sevilla Ms was studied by him, since it is clearly stated in the "Reason for the
Undertaking," found only in the Sevilla Ms and used by Bolton, that Fages made a
journey to the Bay region a year after the Portolá expedition [see text, pp. 39–40, for
the full text of the "Reason for the Undertaking"].

However, in 1911 the Fages diary of 1770 was definitely a discovery, so much so,
apparently, that Irving Berdine Richman in his *California Under Spain and Mexico*
(published ahead of Bolton's article in the Academy *Publications*) included a translation of the diary by a Miss Emma Helen Blair in the Appendix. Richman did not include the Spanish text for the very good reason that he did not have access to it. He
had been provided with a typewritten transcript of the diary through Bolton's scholarly
generosity. Richman did not include, either, any indication of where or how he had
access to the diary. See Charles Edward Chapman in *A History of California: The
Spanish Period* (1930), Appendix, p. 502, item #14.

When the famous Bolton *Guide* appeared (1913) it listed the 1770 diary but not the
one of 1772, though both are found in the same archive, section, and volume [see
*Guide to the Materials for the History of the United States in the Principal Archives of
Mexico*, p. 168].

The present writer first encountered the Fages diary of 1772 while working through
the microfilm cited above. Having recognized the document, the writer consulted the
index to the Bolton Papers compiled in 1961–62 by Vivian C. Fisher [C-B. 840 Part
I: *Key to the Research Materials of Herbert Eugene Bolton*] and found reference to the
diary in the Alta California section, Item #94. This item, in Folder #3, contains a
typescript of the Fages diary and a few pages of translation, some typed and some in
Dr. Bolton's handwriting.

Next, an effort was made to bring together any references to possible uses of the
1772 diary. Here may be noted:

1) The first mention of the diary is found in the Academy of Pacific Coast History
Publications cited above (1911).

2) A later mention of the diary is found in Bolton's *Crespi* (1927), not accompanied
with a citation.

3) Mention of the diary in Rudolph Herman Drewes, *Pedro Fages, California
Pioneer* (M.A. Thesis, U.C., 1927). No use made of the diary; no statement as to
where or if the diary had been seen, or from whence had come information about it.

4) First specific mention of the diary *as a discovery*, and also first use of a part of the
diary, the *Nota*, a kind of addendum, which is not a part of the diary proper in specific
subject matter, though physically a part of the document, in *CHSQ*, vol. X, No. 3,
(September 1931), in Bolton's article entitled "In the South San Joaquin Ahead of
Garcés." The entire *Nota* is used in this article. The location of the 1772 diary is not
revealed.

5) In 1935 the Kern County Historical Society published the same article which
had appeared in 1931 in the *CHSQ*, as "An Address Delivered Before the Kern County
Historical Society in May, 1931" [*sic*]. Again, there is no statement about the diary's
location.

6) The *Nota* is referred to in H. I. Priestley, *A Historical, Political, and Natural*

pared the first known map of the Pacific Coast which showed the penetration of the land by two estuaries. The new map, known familiarly as the "Crespí" map, but probably not prepared by him, is drawn so as to reconcile the concept of an outer bay containing the farallones (Cabrera Bueno's and Cermeño's Port of San Francisco) with the newly discovered inner Bay, which the map's own Description, inscribed within a floral design, refers to as the "main part of the Famous Port and River of San Francisco."[63]

The explorers, Fages and Crespí among them, knew that Cabrera's port was supposed to have an entrance to the interior and that this entrance lay somewhere above Point San Pedro (then called *Punta de Almejas*) and below Point Reyes. The map as drawn brings these points close together so as to inclose the seven Farallones. The "good entrance" (*buena entrada*) of Cabrera Bueno and the *boca* or *bocana* of Fages and Crespí, the present Golden Gate, become the same. The great inner estuary, as well as San Pablo Bay, and the "River of San Francisco" then become the *important* part of the entire complex.[64]

Description of California by Pedro Fages . . . (1937), where Priestley cites Bolton's use of the *Nota* in the Kern County paper. For some reason, Priestley does not mention the previous publication of the article in the *CHSQ*. Also Priestley makes no mention concerning the possible location of the diary, though in one place in his Introduction (note #2, p. xi) he asserts that much Fages material is still in the *Archivo Nacional*.

7) In Priestley's *Franciscan Explorations in California* (1946), edited by Dr. Lillian Estelle Fisher, and posthumously published [Dr. Priestley died in 1944], one finds for the first time anywhere the complete citation for the 1772 Fages diary, including its location in *AGN*. It is probable that Dr. Fisher had access to the Bolton typescript; the microfilm now in Bancroft Library was not available until June, 1951 [Mrs. V. C. Fisher checked the microfilm acquisition records to provide this information]. It appears to the writer that the diary might have been used as supportive to entries in Crespí's diary for March 26 and 27, 1772, but not otherwise.

8) Alan K. Brown, "The Various Journals of Juan Crespí" in *The Americas*, XXI, No. 4 (April, 1965), refers to the Fages diary, and his comments, pp. 388–389, should be studied for the comparisons and differences he notes between the Crespí and Fages accounts of their exploration.

A translation of the diary will appear in the *California Historical Society Quarterly* in 1969, the material having already been submitted to Dr. Manuel P. Servín, editor of the *Quarterly*. This publication, and uses which have been made of the diary in this volume, will be viewed by readers, it is hoped, as an effort to complete a project which Dr. Bolton began many years ago but never completed.

[63] See Appendix for a photo-copy of the "Crespí" map and a copy of the Spanish "Description" [left side of map] with its English translation.

[64] See Appendix, "The Mystery of the Crespí Map".

Yet, Father Crespí himself, in his own Diary upon which the map is based, believed that the "true port of San Francisco" had not been reached, and his prayer-like comment near the end of the official Diary can only be interpreted to mean that he hoped the policy-makers would desist from further efforts to go farther to the north, and would instead elect to use the newly-discovered inner port for the new foundations.

Father Serra, writing several months after the return of the expedition, explained to Father Rafael Verger, Guardian of the San Fernando College, that " . . . the evident result [of the expedition] is . . . from here, it is impossible to reach the Port of San Francisco by land. You will see the diary and the map, and you will understant how and why. Your Reverence, along with the most excellent gentleman and the venerable discretorium, will have to decide what steps are to be taken in the matter, and when, although as far as I can see, the situation in these parts here is more important. It is far better to consolidate what we have begun than to reach out for further acquisitions."[65]

If Father Serra's stated position in this 8 August letter is taken at face value, we must recognize that he arrived at it only in the firm belief that the "true port of San Francisco" was, for the time being, unattainable. Moreover, Serra's expression of disappointment in the results of the expedition shows that he did not accept the idea which Father Crespí had expressed, namely, that perhaps the "new" port was adequate. In retrospect it would seem possible to consider Serra's attitude as expressive of an unimaginative nature. However, it seems more likely that Serra was expressing his utter determination to accept nothing but the ultimate achievement, that of founding a mission of San Francisco, "our Father, in his port" (*nuestro Padre, en su Puerto*).

The better to understand Serra's motivation and attitude one should recall that he had come to California on the orders of Gálvez, but once there had worked zealously as was always his wont in forwarding the interests of the mission program. In Lower California, after Gálvez had announced his intention of establishing Spanish control over Upper California, Serra had developed a

---

[65] Antonine Tibesar, O.F.M., ed., *Writings of Junipero Serra* (Washington: Academy of American Franciscan History, 1956), Vol. I, letter #22.

fixed notion, almost obsessive in nature, about the founding of a San Francisco mission. Early in the Gálvez program Serra began to set aside requirements for the new mission. With reference to the vestments for high Mass he noted in a number of his letters that he was keeping one set, "the best of all . . . for our Father, San Francisco."[66]

From August, 1772 until June, 1776, Father Serra held to the belief that the "true port" could not be reached; however, after the explorations of the peninsula by Anza, during the Second Anza Expedition, Serra admitted, as we shall see, that all his misgivings were dispelled and that the "true Harbor of St. Francis" had been found.[67]

If any individual of influence can be singled out for the special part he took in providing a direct interest in the new port, it is probably Father Rafael Verger, the Franciscan Guardian. Verger had a critical attitude anyway toward California events. His first impressions of the California developments seem somewhat negative. He recognized the great difficulties faced by mariners in making the California coastal voyage. In a letter of 27 August, 1771, to his friend in Court, Manuel Lanz de Casafonda, Verger speaks of the harassment of shipping by winds so terrible they might have come from the lower regions, and he noted that "if our monarch is not very desirous of establishing himself in those ports I have mentioned, it would be better for the conquest to proceed by regular degrees, for in this way it would cost less and accomplish more."[68]

At the same time Verger also informed Casafonda that he worried greatly lest the missions were being "founded for show" and that the Franciscans would then receive blame in the event of failures.[69] Further, he stated (27 September 1771) that from advices sent him by Father Benito Cambón, which would be very important for Casafonda's understanding of what Monterey is, that "strictly speaking, and according to what hydrographers teach us,

---

[66] Father Serra's special interest in San Francisco appears throughout his writings, but good examples can be found in *ibid.*, letters #11, #19, #20, and #21 (from February 1770, through June 1771).

[67] See pp. 85–86, text.

[68] Bolton Papers, Bancroft Library. Alta California, Item #91, Folder #57, Verger to Casafonda, 27 August 1771.

[69] *Ibid.*, Folder #58, Verger to Casafonda, 28 August 1771.

this [Monterey] is neither a port nor a bay but a cove with less protection than that at Ocoa [on the Island of Española in the Caribbean], since it has only a short roadstead in which not more than three or four packets can be anchored safely and even at present they are anchored with four anchors as on the most unprotected shore. This is the strict truth. San Diego is a port in the real meaning of the word. . . . It seemed best to me not to omit this information because I have heard this port Monterey valued too highly . . . "[70]

Father Cambón's ideas about Monterey as a port were evidently accepted by Guardian Verger because in December 1771 he repeated the slur on Monterey, saying, "It is declared that Monterey is not a good port, [and now the additional thought] and that San Francisco may be a very good one, but it is necessary to explore its entrance and bottom" (that is, to learn its depth).[71]

After the Fages-Crespí exploration of 1772 Verger wrote again to Casafonda, saying: "Knowing the keen interest you have shown in the new discovery of the Port and Great River of San Francisco . . . [I send you] the rudimentary form of the map I have sketched, guided by the observations and information communicated to me by Father Predicador Fray Juan Crespí." In this same document Verger revealed a sure sense of the importance of the entire Bay region. The port would have adequate depth for ships; this was indicated by the presence of whales in the bay. There was timber—groves of oak trees—and a great plain ten leagues long and five to six leagues broad in the southern part of the estuary. Verger insisted on the utter necessity that the Bay be occupied "because of the grave danger to the Crown of Spain which would result if some foreign nation were to establish itself in the port. They then would build ships in the great estuary mentioned and move into the interior as they wished, since the land is so extensive and fertile; they could establish colonies and impede our conquests, and even take possession of that which is now subject to our Catholic Monarch."[72]

---

[70] *Ibid.*, Folder #67, Verger to Casafonda, 27 September 1771.

[71] *Ibid.*, Item #95, Folder #23, Verger memorandum to Viceroy, 23 December 1771.

[72] *Ibid.*, Folder #30, Verger to Casafonda, 27 December 1772.

On the same day that the Guardian sent this information and opinion with his prepared map to Casafonda he also despatched a map, a memorial, and Crespí's Diary to the Viceroy who, in turn, sent the map, the memorial, and a copy of the Diary to Minister Arriaga. Thus, the Crown, through the Franciscan Guardian, Rafael Verger, was getting the message about San Francisco Bay from two directions, and it seems clear that in Father Verger the Bay had a high-echelon booster.[73]

Meanwhile, somewhat earlier in the year 1772, Viceroy Bucareli had received the first petition (dated 2 May 1772) from Captain Juan Bautista de Anza, a presidial commander at Tubac, Sonora, requesting permission to attempt the opening of a Sonora-California land route.[74] The Viceroy's response to the Anza petition was one of desiring to go slowly. He spelled out his "cautious approach" in a letter to the Minister of the Indies, Julián de Arriaga, 27 October 1772, stating that "better results have always been obtained by acquisitions that have been made gently by means of the missionaries than by those obtained by force of arms." More information was also needed, he said, and waiting until next year would give the opportunity for decision-making to His Majesty.[75]

On the same day of his report on the Anza petition Viceroy Bucareli sent another despatch to the Indies Minister wherein he expressed annoyance at having failed to receive sufficiently detailed information about such an important subject as the exploration of the Port of San Francisco so that he could not say with certainty that the "true" port was known. He particularly blamed Captain Fages for having filed a brief report, and stated that he had requested additional information. If at about the same time or

---

[73] Item #2089 in the invaluable Charles Edward Chapman, *Catalogue of Materials in the Archivo General de Indias [AGI] for the History of the Pacific Coast and the American Southwest* (Berkeley, 1919). Microfilm, Bancroft Library, *AGI*, Audiencia de Guadalajara 512, Roll III.

[74] Bucareli took the oath of office before the Royal *Audiencia* on September 23, 1771. Bernard E. Bobb, *The Viceregency of Antonio María Bucareli in New Spain, 1771–1779* (University of Texas, 1962), p. 24. Anza's petition is dated Tubac [Sonora] May 2, 1772. Bolton, *Anza*, V, p. 2 ff.

[75] *Ibid.*, p. 41 ff. See Bobb, *op. cit.*, Ch. 6, "The California Colonization", p. 162. Professor Bobb points out that the Viceroy's question, "How much will it cost?", was part of his "cautious approach."

earlier the Viceroy also received Father Serra's interpretation of Bay area geography (the letter of 8 August), his need for more information was certainly plain.[76]

It should be carefully noted that the Viceroy's reaction to the Anza petition and his complaint about lack of information preceded his receipt of the Crespí material and that, furthermore, when the Crespí information arrived the Viceroy simply sent it on to Spain. The truth of the matter is that Bucareli was in his "low ebb" phase of involvement in the Upper California program, and this attitude remained his from December 1772 into the Summer of 1773. Indeed, it appears likely from the record that had Bucareli not received ideas and pressure from a number of sources, the Upper California enterprise might have been given up.

It is ironic that the Viceroy's pessimism should have stemmed in part from the information and misinformation he was receiving about the conflict between the San Fernando College Franciscans and the military in Upper California. The Church and the Military were Spain's twin forces in such a matter as the California enterprise and were expected to cooperate and not to contend with each other. Yet Bucareli had to report to Minister Arriaga, 27 December 1772, that the "remedy for those difficulties" (not only between the military and the missionaries, it should be noted) had been the first object of his attention since he had taken command of the Kingdom of New Spain.[77]

In January 1773 the Viceroy received Royal Instructions which included a program of strengthening the northern defenses. "Finally", read the document, "His Majesty directs particular attention, as the Regulation and Instruction indicate at length, to the old and new establishments of the Californias, for in their possession rests the extension of his dominions, the security of that Province [of New Spain], and, above all, the propagation of the Faith and the light of the Gospel; take his Royal order as the special charge of Your Excellency so that the said establishments be

---

[76] See page 44, text. Bucareli's complaint about insufficient information is found in Chapman, Item #2044, microfilm, Bancroft Library, *AGI*, Aud. de Guad. 416, Roll III.

[77] Chapman, Item #2086, microfilm, *ibid.*

supported and supplied that they will not decline, but will rather grow by means of the voluntary conversion of the Indians."[78]

The Crown's concern was not a reaction to any proposals or information supplied by Viceroy Bucareli; he had been in office only since September 1771 and was, as noted, somewhat confounded by information he had received from and about Upper California. Rather, it was the predecessor of Bucareli, Marqués de Croix, the collaborator with Gálvez, who had provided the incentive for the Crown's new concern.[79]

Despite the Crown's instructions, the Viceroy now responded with a letter to Minister Arriaga, 24 February 1773, which expressed a sense of dejection at the prospects for California. He wrote: "The discord which has developed between Captain Don Pedro de Faxes [*sic*] and the pious missionaries; the repeated desertions among the soldiers; the various applications for assistance made by the latter; these reveal the deplorable situation and near ruin of the new establishments of the Californias whose conquest was obtained at the cost of immense cost and labor." He reported further that his efforts to remedy the situation had been of little avail.[80]

Other influences now began to bear upon Viceroy Bucareli. A second petition was prepared by Anza (dated 7 March 1773), and Father Serra arrived in the capital to present his suggestions to the Viceroy for improving the government of the missions, which he did on 13 March 1773.[81] By April Serra had also presented a

---

[78] The Crown's orders received by Bucareli in January, 1773, are found in the *Cédulas* of 25 September and 12 October 1772. The second of these is cited in Bobb, *op. cit.*, p. 163, and footnote 24, where there is also found an excellent evaluation of the pressure being exerted on the Viceroy from Spain. For both documents, see microfilm, Bancroft Library, *AGN*, Mexico, *Reales Cédulas* [*RC*], Vols. 102 (2)–103 (1), #97 and #104, Reel #56.

[79] Arriaga to Bucareli, 25 September 1772, *ibid.*, #97, refers to information which had been received by the Crown from the Marqués de Croix, in a despatch dated 20 September 1771. Because of insufficient time for their printing, copies of the new regulation did not go out at this time; however, the 12 October *cédula* mentions forty examples being sent.

[80] Chapman, Item #2177. Microfilm, Bancroft Library, *AGI*, Aud. de Guad., 514, Roll I.

[81] For the second Anza petition, see Bolton, *Anza*, V. For a full discussion of Serra's meeting with Bucareli see Geiger, *Serra*, I, Chapter XLIII, "A Bill of Particulars".

lengthy and potent list of arguments in favor of keeping the San
Blas establishment as a base for supply ships, since he had heard
rumors that mule pack-trains were to be substituted for the maritime supply line.[82]

During the same Spring of 1773 the Minister Plenipotentiary of
the Spanish King to the Russian Court in St. Petersburg, the
Conde de Lacy, had sent a number of despatches to Madrid, telling
of Russian exploration in the North Pacific. It was feared by Spain
that the Russians had actually reached the "northern coasts of the
Californias."[83] The information possessed by the Spanish authorities was forwarded to Viceroy Bucareli with specific instructions
through a Royal Order (*cédula*) dated 11 April 1773, Madrid, that
the Viceroy take appropriate steps to determine how far the Russians had advanced. This order and the alarming reports reached
Bucareli in July; his acknowledgement of the Royal Cédula
and the reports, along with a preliminary outline of his plans of
action, are found in a document addressed to Minister Arriaga on
July 27, 1773.[84]

Bucareli was able to state categorically that there were no
foreign establishments between Cape San Lucas and Monterey;
that in recent times no ships had been sighted along the coast except the Philippine ship (the Manila Galleon), and the supply ships
which plied between San Blas and Monterey and San Diego. He
spoke also of the new regulation, being forwarded in another document, to support the old and new California establishments, and of
the projected maritime expedition to be headed by Juan Pérez to
explore the coasts north of Monterey.[85]

Therein is also found a listing and analysis of Serra's points, which Father Geiger
terms a legal brief, called the *Representación*. See also Tibesar, *op. cit.*, letter #28.

[82] Geiger, *ibid.*, 381–82, where Serra is credited with saving San Blas; both the
Viceroy and Madrid accepted Serra's arguments.

[83] Chapman, *Catalogue*, Items #2038, #2044, #2126, #2162, and #2197, covering
the period from 27 October 1772 to 19 March 1773.

[84] *Ibid.*, Items #2209, #2210, and #2211. Bucareli's response to the reports about
the Russians is found in Item #2337.

[85] *Ibid.*, Item #2337. See also Vernon Dale Tate, "The Juan Pérez Expedition to
the Northwest Coast, 1774" (unpublished M.A. thesis, Berkeley, 1930) for a well-
documented account of this subject. Tate considers the fear of Russia as the diplomatic
basis for the Pérez voyage. Chapman, *History of California: The Spanish Period*, Ch.

At the same time Bucareli sent a letter to his friend, General Alejandro O'Reilly, which falls into the realm of unofficial correspondence, where, as one man speaking to another, he could express his sentiments simply and directly. In this particular letter, 27 July 1773, Viceroy Bucareli stated that the principal purpose of the new regulation was to check the designs of the Russians.[86]

Thus, the events of Spring, culminating in the Viceroy's response in the Summer of 1773, were a turning point in the history of Spanish California. Bucareli now became a direct heir to the heritage of "defensive expansion" established by Visitor-General Joseph de Gálvez.

Other events of what might be called an aggressive program followed in rapid succession. A dominant purpose with Father Serra for his visit to the capital had been his wish to convince the Viceroy to remove Captain Pedro Fages from his command. Fages was replaced by Captain Fernando Javier de Rivera y Moncada who was called out of retirement and named military commander of Upper California.

XX, "Russian and English Aggressions in the Pacific Northwest" should be consulted with reference to the entire concept of Spanish "defensive expansion" as a response to a "foreign threat."

[86] *Ibid.*, Item #2342. See Chapman, "The Founding of San Francisco" in *The Pacific Ocean in History, etc.*, H. M. Stephens and H. E. Bolton, eds. (1917), pp. 376–377 and footnote for an interesting discussion of Bucareli's private correspondence with General Alejandro O'Reilly, much of which concerned Bucareli's concern with the "Russian menace."

6

The Opening of the Sonora–California Land Route by Anza

Captain Rivera was appointed to his new command on 14 August 1773, and three days later received a general instruction which read, in part: "The Commandant will proceed wholly in consideration that the object of the New Establishments is to advance the spiritual conquest, and therefore the extension of the dominions of the King. In view of the fact that the Port of San Francisco, though already reconnoitered, requires further examination, the Commandant shall immediately dispose the proper means to effect it, for the purpose of deliberating in accord with the Father President upon whether it is possible to found a mission there."[87]

Then followed the very important 9 September *Council of War*

---

[87] Alan K. Brown, "Rivera at San Francisco: A Journal of Exploration, 1774" in *CHSQ*, XLI, No. 4 (December, 1962). This is an exceptionally perceptive article consisting in a translation of the Rivera Diary, with an Introduction and footnotes. Brown quotes part of the Paragraph 18 of the Instructions to Rivera, beginning with the words, "In view of the fact . . . etc." The full paragraph is quoted in the present work from the microfilm, Bancroft Library, *AGI*, Aud. de Guad., 514, Roll II (Chapman Item #2350). The Diary may be studied in *ibid.*, Roll III (Chapman Item #2761).

Father Palóu must have heard about the Rivera Instructions because in December, 1773, in his Report to the Viceroy [Palóu acting for Serra during the latter's visit to Mexico] he states: " . . . we have had in mind going to examine again the shore of the Gulf of the Farallones in the direction that faces towards the port of Monterey, and if a place be found suitable for that mission [San Francisco], not too far from the beach, to proceed with its founding, since it is not known with certainty where the harbor is, for only on that Gulf of the Farallones, when the bark can go to examine it to make soundings, can it be founded; and in case the harbor is on the other side of the Gulf, if your Excellency should judge it proper, launches can go to found another." See Palóu, *Historical Memoirs*, III, p. 235. Rivera reached Monterey in May, 1774 (see text, p. 54).

wherein approval was given to Anza to make his exploration, and next a letter went out to Rivera on the 19th of September ordering him to provide Anza with support. Shortly later, 26 September, the Viceroy wrote a long despatch to Minister Arriaga telling him of his action program: the Anza plan, "which perhaps had its origin in a similar request made in the year 1737 by the father of him who presents it", would, if successful, not only more strongly secure San Diego and Monterey, it would also promote the reconnaissance "of that vast coast"; Serra had been called in prior to the Council meeting, had expressed the opinion that the project was possible and useful "and as a preliminary to other explorations if, communication by land to Monterey having been opened, use might be made of the troops who should effect it, in order that the coast might be followed and a more careful examination made of the port of San Francisco and beyond it, at the same time that an effort is being made to effect the same investigation by sea.

"Since the president of the missions knows the country," continued the Viceroy in his letter to the Minister, "because he has lived there two years, for he was one of these who effected the occupation, and who, moved by his zeal, came to this capital to promote what was best for the ordinance which was drawn up for the old and the new establishments of California, and since his suggestion may forward the desire of his Majesty that efforts be made to investigate the new explorations of the Russians, I assembled the council of war and exchequer on the 9th of the present month. There, after an account was given of the file of documents, it was decided to grant to Captain Anza the aid of twenty volunteers from his presidio . . ."[88]

Thus, by September, 1773, the Viceroy's office had given support to a new exploration of San Francisco Bay to be carried out by Captain Rivera, and to Anza's plan to open a land route to California. Captain Anza had initiated the idea of the exploration, a heritage from his father, as the Viceroy had noted,[89] and Father Serra's support of the plan was decisive for its acceptance by the

---

[88] Anza documents are in Bolton, *Anza*, V, unless otherwise specified.

[89] The senior Anza had written to the Viceroy, January 14, *1737*, requesting permission to make an exploration of the Colorado River.

Viceroy. And there is clear indication in the Viceroy's remarks to the Minister that the need for securing the defenses of the north coast was a paramount consideration in all that went on in the Council of War.

Captain Rivera's reaction to his orders was one of obvious discomfiture. He had not received the viceregal instructions of 19 September to support Anza until the 11th of October; he then hastened to respond to them in a letter of the 12th. He promised strictly to observe the Viceroy's orders; he offered the opinion that if Anza persisted in his undertaking he would come out between San Diego and the mission of San Gabriel (an excellent judgment); and, then, introducing a note of poignancy, he wrote: "This, most excellent Sir, is an enterprise which I thought to be important, even when I was in the midst of the difficulties presented to us by the long journey of the expedition [in 1769] and by the poverty of that extensive country, and there was a time when I planned to propose it if occasion should offer, but it having happened before this opportunity came to me that I heard of the pretension of this captain, I was greatly pleased."[90]

Rivera did not reach Monterey until 23 May 1774; he assumed command from Pedro Fages two days later. Anza, however, had already by then made his famous march from Sonora to California, and had been a visitor in Monterey from the 18th to the 22nd of April. During that time he had conferred with Father Francisco Palóu, and the two men had dreamed of a bright future for California.[91] One mention was made of San Francisco Bay during their discussions; Anza proposed that the Manila Galleon make a stop there or at Monterey. Since the Palóu-Anza meeting preceded Anza's own exploration of the Bay, it is likely that Anza's reference was to Cabrera's port.

Father Palóu reported his meeting with Anza in a letter to the Guardian, dated at Mission San Carlos, Monterey, April 22, 1774.

---

[90] Rivera to Bucareli, Guadalajara, 12 October 1773. Without making it a central theme, additional information is provided below concerning the famous Anza-Rivera differences.

[91] See the beautifully written chapter in Bolton, *Anza*, I, "Anza and Palóu See Visions."

The letter was sent via Captain Anza. "The Captain", wrote Palóu, "as soon as he reaches his presidio will go to give an account of his expedition to his Excellency. He has promised me that he will go to see your Reverence [at the College of San Fernando in Mexico City] and give you a report of these missions and of the projects that he is taking to propose to his Excellency for the good of these new conquests, in which I hope that your Reverence will cooperate as far as you can."[92]

Except for an unanticipated delay, things worked out pretty much as Father Palóu's report to the Guardian indicated that they might. Anza was prevented from going directly from Sonora to the capital because of the presidial inspection tour then in progress under direction of adjutant inspector Don Antonio Bonilla. The latter ordered Anza to journey from his presidio of Tubac to the Terrenate presidio and remain in command there until relief arrived from New Mexico. Anza wrote the Viceroy from Terrenate and explained his delay.[93]

The Viceroy, greatly irked by Bonilla's action, wrote to Minister Arriaga: "Being convinced, as I am, that there is no project of greater importance in this province today than the one which Ansa has just executed with such care, and that my orders to him to come to this capital as soon as he should have completed it being known to Bonilla, he ought not to have detained him for any reason, I have found it necessary to inform the commandante inspector, Don Hugo Oconor, how annoying this act of Bonilla has been to me, so that he may let him know about it, and to instruct the governor ad interim of the province to release Ansa immediately, so that he may begin his journey at once."[94]

Before Anza could reach Mexico and make his direct report to Viceroy Bucareli, the Viceroy had received yet another report about Russian explorations in the North Pacific. Thus, when Anza's Diary was placed in Bucareli's hands on 13 November

---

[92] *Ibid.*, V.

[93] *Ibid.*, document XXXV, letter of 8 June 1774

[94] *Ibid.*, document XLV, Mexico 27 August 1774. See also *ibid.*, I, for a detailed description of Anza's return journey in the Chapters "Up the Gila and Home" and "Rewards" (XXV and XXVI, respectively).

1774, the juxtaposition of events was more favorable than it had ever been for the carrying through of the plan to occupy the Port of San Francisco. Indeed, four days after delivering his Diary, Anza, on request, readied a rather detailed plan for what was to become his second expedition. And on the 26th of November 1774 the Viceroy sent a long despatch to Minister Arriaga concerned largely with the Juan Pérez expedition which had returned to San Blas after having reached the 55th parallel.[95] In its last paragraph on its seventh page this despatch also informed the Minister that Naval Lieutenant Don Diego de Manrique, commander of the packet-ship *El Príncipe*, as soon as he had unloaded provisions and supplies at Monterey, was to continue his voyage for the carrying out of an exploration of the Port of San Francisco. " . . . I hold the occupation of [that Port] to be indispensable," wrote Bucareli, "and to effect it Captain Don Juan Bautista de Anza, who is today in this capital, will return to Sonora to plan a second *entrada*, conducting troops required to support the two new missions, and as a symbol of defense in that port."[96]

In another document of the same date Bucareli wrote: " . . . it now appears to me necessary to explore the land still further and to establish a presidio at the port of San Francisco, which by all means ought to be occupied to support our conquests in that region, as I explain in another letter of this date . . . treating of the arrival of the frigate *Santiago* [Captain Pérez], and I am now planning a second expedition, to be carried out by Captain Don Juan Bauptista de Ansa, with adequate assistance and a larger number of people, so that thirty of the men may remain in San Francisco as escort for two new missions and as a sign of protection in that port, taking also cattle and horses to aid with their progeny in the support of the new establishments."[97]

---

[95] See p. 63, text, for mention of the Pérez voyage.

[96] Microfilm, Bancroft Library, *AGI*, Papeles de Estado 20, Roll II, Bucareli to Arriaga. See pp. 63 ff., text, for the nautical exploration of San Francisco Bay by Captain Ayala who replaced Captain Manrique because of the latter's illness.

[97] Bolton, *Anza*, V, pp. 195–196, Bucareli to Arriaga, 26 November 1774. See Appendix 6, "Council of War and Royal Exchequer" (Mexico, December 16, 1774).

7

The Rivera–Palóu Exploration
of the Peninsula: 1774

It should be remembered that earlier the Viceroy had ordered the Rivera-Palóu expedition to explore the "Port and River of San Francisco." Yet at the very time that Captain Rivera was able to begin his exploration the Viceroy had already reached a decision finally to establish settlements on that Port. One wonders if, had communications been easy and rapid, the Rivera-Palóu expedition might have been cancelled in view of the new developments.

Rivera and Palóu proceeded on their way (23d November) without, of course, being aware of the Viceroy's decisions. Captain Rivera was very conscious of his instructions; namely, to bring back very accurate information about the region, including the rivers seen by Fages. The expression, River of San Francisco, had been added to the geographical concepts of the time, and is used in all the documents after the 1772 exploration by Fages whenever reference is made to the Port of San Francisco.

In his entry for Sunday, November 27, Rivera wrote: "We heard Mass, and in order to give time for the shelters to air, dinner was ordered to be eaten early and followed by the day's march: and thus it was done. At twelve o'clock we started off on the same course; and were our efforts directed to a straight march to the rivers, here is where we should take the way straight to the north, passing by the end of the southeastern arm of the harbor. But as the fundamental and basic thing is the harbor itself, and, of this, its gateway, entrance and exit: even though it might be at the cost of later having to retrace a great stretch of country in order to take the way to the rivers from here, *I continued on to the northwest in search of the very mouth of the harbor.*" (Italics, T.E.T.)

On the 28th the expedition camped on San Francisquito Creek somewhere on the site of modern Palo Alto and both Rivera and Palóu considered this the best location for a mission in the entire peninsula area. Rivera said it was the best site because "I passed through there at the time of the first expedition [1769] looking for heathens. The plain is spacious, abounding in grasses and acorn-bearing live oaks, and is the nearest to the mouth or entrance of this harbor that a foundation can be made: for true though it is that there are water and good grass by that entrance, it is equally the case that there is neither firewood there nor a single stick to build with. I have seen that terrain beforehand, and speak from what I know. Here where we crossed this same creek a tall cross has been set up, with its arms fastened by an iron spike, beside an Indian trail."[98]

And Palóu also pointed out the advantages of the site for a mission and then said that when they were erecting the cross they were "fixing in it our good hopes to found on the same spot a church dedicated to my Seraphic Father San Francisco, whom I name as intermediary in order that his Divine Majesty may grant that I may see it in my day, and that I may see reduced to our holy faith the great heathendom which inhabits this vicinity."[99]

On November 30th they camped near a small-sized lake from where they could see the harbor and also a "high, bare mountain, lying as it seems to me northwest and east. Tomorrow I think to climb it", wrote Rivera, "in order to search out the place where these waters enter, *which I have never really seen.*" (Italics, T.E.T.) Rain and fog delayed Rivera on the 1st of December, but finally on the 2nd he with four soldiers climbed the mountain, which was

---

[98] The quotations are from Rivera's Journal in Brown, *loc. cit.* On the matter of Rivera's estimate of the peninsula's potentialities, Brown says: "If the ostensible chronology of the entries in the journal translated here can be trusted, Rivera had already decided that the tip of the San Francisco peninsula was no fit place for a settlement before, as he puts it, really seeing it. In fact, his opinion must have been based on a view from the mountains back of present Millbrae in 1769 . . . " Or, it may be added, from oral reports from members of the Ortega expedition.

[99] Bolton, *Anza*, II. Palóu's Diary, known as (I), p. 395 ff.

obviously San Bruno Mountain, and from where he described his view.

"I saw the meeting or fork of the two arms, one drawing to the north and the one we had kept on our right that goes to the southeast. The mainland between these arms rises at no great distance back from the shore, making as it seemed to me a sort of point, I can't say precisely what; at the same place, the northern estuary turns inland so sharply that it is soon covered to view from the height. I saw two islands [presently named Angel and Yerba Buena], and there is a sort of bay there. I perceived where the entrance might be, but could not make it out; for this reason I descended in search of it; and travelling a stretch of a league and a half, stopped on top of a peak where from a distance of half a league I discovered part of the mouth, which it seemed to me must be a scant quarter-league wide."

Rivera had to turn back to camp because he saw a great sand dune lying between the peak and the mouth, and the animals were tired. On December 4th he led his expedition on a "northwesterly course" because "It was my purpose", he wrote, "to tread the beach and halt upon the point at the very mouth of the harbor, for though I saw it at so short a distance as said above, it happened that on my return I found myself less than satisfied."

In the context of the diary there is a sense of pride discernible in what Rivera now reported: "I succeeded in treading the beach, and came to stand upon the very point on the south side, the one with the three rocks. Around this point, within the mouth, there are other rocks awash at the land's edge; they show at low tide, and some of them must uncover when it is full; if not, their position will be shown by broken water, and they will be no danger to vessels, being by the shore and the rest of the entrance left open and free. The land to the northwest on the other side lies parallel to that described above; there is a red cliff running out in a point, with a black rock; to the northwest at the foot is the cove and shelter, and along that piece of coast several groups of cliffs are seen. The width of the entrance must be a short quarter-league; it looks westward, and nearly opposite it lies one of the groups of the Farallones. The mouth continues inland to the east in the shape of a narrow pass or roadway, and at another quarter-league's distance are two more points, closing in a little without straitening the entrance. Near by them was a small seachop raised, which, for all that, I did not suppose indicated a shoal, but rather that it was caused by the strong current meeting a stiff wind. Close past these comes the separation of the northern and southeastern arms; there is some sort of a bay; and directly behind the aforesaid points is seen a sizable island, with the separating mainland at its back.

"Between the above-described cove and Point Reyes, which ends west-northwest, will, I am persuaded, be found the harbor read of in the *History of Californias* and in *Cabrera Bueno*, and also that these waters here treated were first discovered by our first expedition journey [1769]. A cross was set up on the point."

Rivera's surmise, just quoted, is the most direct reference in any of the documents up to his time that San Francisco Bay was a new discovery, found by the Portolá expedition of which Rivera had been a member, and that it was not an inner bay or estuary connected with the bay of Cabrera Bueno.[100] It has been noted that although Father Crespí and Sergeant Ortega had earlier recognized the magnificence of the inland estuary, they yet had not dissociated it from the "port of San Francisco."

Rivera's companion, Father Palóu, now recognized that there must be two ports, but he continued to cling to the letter of the Visitor's decree that the "port of San Francisco" be settled, and "San Francisco" had not yet been found! Here is Father Palóu's solution to this vexatious problem. "Although I have said there are cliffs on each side of the channel, and that between them the bay debouches into the Gulf [of the Farallones], yet, after passing the narrowest part of the channel the beach on the north side is low. And it is the same on this south side, and there would be nothing to prevent launches from crossing and loading and unloading, and even horses, for the purpose of going to Point Reyes, *near which it is said the harbor of San Francisco is* [italics, T.E.T.], for, since the channel is so narrow, it might perhaps be possible for animals to cross in tow of canoes."

---

[100] See Appendix, pp. 126–127, for Father Verger's views on this subject.

After describing the Gulf of the Farallones, as seen from their vantage point, Father Palóu returns to his description of the local scene. "Now that we saw so near at hand the mouth by which the bay is entered, it seemed to us that its width was not more than a quarter of a league, although from a distance it seems wider, for the commander, who had seen it two days previously from the top of a hill, about half a league from it, judged it to be half a league wide. For this reason I am not surprised that when the last expedition saw it from the other side as far as ten leagues away [Crespí and Fages, in 1772], it appeared to them to be about three quarters of a league wide as the diary says. For from the site from which they were looking at it they saw the island and the channels by which the two arms of the estuary enter, and it appeared to them that this stretch of the island and the channels measured the width of the mouth. But we now saw it to be narrow inside, about a quarter of a league, and that it must be of the same width on each side of the island that is in the mouth. *The rest of the islands mentioned in the diary we could not see from the precipitous cliff.* [Italics, T.E.T.]

"Observing that this cliff of the strait or mouth of the estuary of San Francisco is on the point of land, *and that up to the present time no Spaniard nor any Christian had set foot on it* [italics, T.E.T.], the commander and I decided to plant the standard of the holy cross on the summit of it, and we did so, making it of two timbers, and leaving it planted on the spot which may be seen from the beach. This finished, we returned by the same road along the beach, and afterwards by the ridge to the camp, arriving about three."[101]

Captain Rivera now decided to return to Monterey, and he summarized his reasons for making this decision in his entry for December the 5th. "Having undergone the rough weather, the rain and cold wind, and the ground hard going for our beasts, with clouds yet overhead threatening rain; with two days' return march to make down to the end of the arm of the harbor before heading north to the rivers (on which road there are no boats to be found to enable crossing any of the creeks and rivers if they should rise);

---

[101] The date of the march to the harbor entrance was December 4th; the cross was erected on Pt. Lobos, or thereabouts. Had the party proceeded to Fort Point, all three main islands could have been sighted.

and considering the men's battered condition as well as my own bruises—I decided to make my way back to Monterey and leave the rest to be attempted toward the end of March or beginning of April, that being the time when the rains, if they do not stop, draw off somewhat."

The expedition now proceeded south and in the early afternoon of December 5th reached the camp site of the 1769 Portolá expedition in Pedro Valley. They followed the Portolá trail back to Monterey where they arrived on the morning of the 13th of December, 1774.

Captain Rivera and Father Palóu had failed to explore the San Francisco peninsula in the very areas where later were established both the Presidio and Mission San Francisco. Rivera evidently considered the area near the harbor entrance as inhospitable; both men had agreed on the advantages of the San Francisquito site.[102] Despite the opinions of Rivera and Palóu, Father Serra wrote a letter to the Viceroy, dated 8 January 1775, in which he blithely stated that although the explorers had explored only the lesser part of what the map showed of the previous expedition, what they had seen was really the most important part. . . . "since it is the continuation of the line of direction of these missions, which in all cases keeps near the coast. This district too is most suitable for settlement, not only for the above-mentioned reasons, but also *because it brings us nearest to the port we seek* [italics, T.E.T.], that is, taking it for granted that the map-makers are right in placing it near Point Reyes. So with the new exploration, we locate it near the mouth of the estuary, from where by an easy crossing there is no difficulty at all in getting to the opposite bank of the Bay of the Farallones, which comes to a finish with the said point of the port."[103]

---

[102] This squared with Rivera's earlier view, expressed in his letter to Viceroy Croix in 1770. See p. 32, text, and note 48.

[103] Tibesar, *op. cit.*, II, letter #66, Serra to Bucareli.

8

The "San Carlos" and the First Nautical Survey of the Bay: 1775

In the meantime, as we have seen, without reference to the findings of Palóu and Rivera, and now also without the benefit of Serra's opinions—since he did not wait for the former and did not know that the latter was writing—the Viceroy had, in November 1774, decided to send Anza on his second expedition, this one for the purposes of both exploration and colonization.[104]

However, before the second Anza expedition could move into California, a maritime phase of exploration brought the first Spanish vessel into San Francisco Bay and accomplished the first nautical survey of the Bay's farthest reaches. Earlier the Spanish had explored the Pacific coast north of San Francisco Bay through the voyages of Juan Pérez, Bruno de Eceta, and Juan de Bodega y Cuadra, during the period from the summer of 1774 to the spring of 1775. Now in March, 1775, the "packet boat" *San Carlos*, alias *Toison de Oro* (Golden Fleece), under command of Lieutenant of Frigate, Don Manuel de Ayala, left San Blas for Monterey. Captain Ayala was sailing under the same orders which had been given to Lieutenant Diego de Manrique, but that unfortunate man had become mentally deranged and had been replaced by Ayala. The orders called for a survey of the port of San Francisco, once Ayala had unloaded cargo at Monterey and readied his ship for the exploration.

After a disagreeably long voyage of some three months the

---

[104] The chronology of communications illustrates how certain activities which could have reënforced each other were often out of phase because of the time lag.

San Carlos anchored on June 27, 1775, off the Presidio at Monterey. This little vessel, destined to become one of the most famous in California annals, was a ship of one hundred and ninety-three tons, with an overall length of fifty-eight feet, a beam of seventeen feet, and an average draft of eight and one-half feet. She was known as a packet-ship (*paquebot*). She was *snow*-rigged (foremast, mainmast, and trysail).[105] Since the exploration of the harbor was a principal purpose of the voyage, "in order to do this more accurately", wrote Father Palóu, "he [Captain Ayala] had a small *cayuco* built. It was made by the carpenters of the *San Carlos*, on the bank of the Carmelo River, from a large redwood tree that grew on the plain, while the crew unloaded the ship."[106]

During the month the *San Carlos* remained in port in Monterey, Father Serra wrote an enthusiastic letter to Viceroy Bucareli, bearing the date of 2 July 1775. He told in it of having received the joyous news in the letter delivered to him from the ship of the Viceroy's decision to occupy the Port of San Francisco with a fort and two missions. The Viceroy's letter was dated 15 December 1774, and now—in July—the northern frontier learned that Anza would bring colonists from Sonora to found new establishments. There is no clue in Serra's letter that allows us to judge whether his reference to the Port of San Francisco was to the harbor under Point Reyes or the present Bay of San Francisco.

---

[105] Details for the *San Carlos* voyage can be found in Boyd Francis Huff, "The Maritime History of San Francisco Bay" (unpublished Ph.D. thesis, University of California, Berkeley, 1955); Z. S. Eldredge, E. J. Molera, *The March of Portolá and The Log of the San Carlos* (1909); and Bolton, *Palóu's Historical Memoirs*, IV. However, for particular details the Ayala and Cañizáres accounts have been consulted (microfilms, *Bancroft Library*. See specific references in later footnotes). Huff identifies the first anchorage of the *San Carlos* as somewhere off North Beach. See pp. 66 ff. for the present writer's discussion of this question.

[106] Bolton, *Palóu*, IV, p. 5. Also Tibesar, *op. cit.*, II, #80, Serra to Pangua, 24 July 1775. On this date, actually two days ahead of the departure-date of the *San Carlos*, Father Serra wrote to the Guardian, among other things: "The *San Carlos* is now starting for San Francisco, and a number of soldiers are going by land to act as an escort for the launch, as it proceeds along shore to inspect the numerous headlands as marked down in Father Crespí's map. . . ." Serra's reference to a land party as an escort for the launch seems to establish the fact that he had in mind a Crespí map of the Bay. However, the only headlands marked on the map thus far known as the "Crespí" map are two, not several; namely, the Punta de Reyes and the Punta de Almejas. See map, Appendix, and discussion of the "Crespí" map, under the title: The Mystery of the "Crespí" Map.

Serra had already selected Father Professor Fray Francisco Palóu and Father Preacher Fray Pedro Benito Cambón for the San Francisco mission. He noted that Captain Ayala was to make arrangements with the Captain Commandant, Rivera, so that a number of soldiers would go by land as a supporting force for the ship. Serra expressed the thought that the whole plan was an excellent one, but, as he states, he added an item to it himself, namely, ". . . that Fathers Palóu and Peña should go with the troops, not only in order to gather fresh information about the country they are appointed to take care of . . . but to be with the soldiers."[107]

Father Palóu in his comments on the plan stated that Señor Ayala would construct, by means of the crew, a house to serve as a lodging on the arrival of the people of the land expedition who were accompanying Don Juan de Anza.[108]

Plans for the supporting party were disrupted by the threat of an Indian uprising in San Diego which had forced Commandant Rivera to send soldiers there. It was agreed that when these troops returned they would proceed to the port. These arrangements having been made, the *San Carlos* weighed anchor on July 26th, though she had to be kedged out of the bay to catch wind on on the day following, through use of the ship's long-boat. After a very arduous voyage she arrived off the entrance to San Francisco Bay on the 5th of August 1775, in the early morning. The Captain ordered the pilot, Don José Cañizáres, to enter the Bay in the ship's launch, to find a good anchorage. Cañizáres carried out his orders, entered the inner Bay, and was, therefore, the first European to navigate the waters of the Bay, and the ship's long-boat (*lancha*) was the first craft to pass through what later became known as the Golden Gate.

In the late afternoon, with night beginning to close in and the launch not having returned, Captain Ayala decided to take the *San Carlos* into the Bay. He made extremely slow progress against an outgoing tide, but a favorable wind held and he worked his way

---

[107] Tibesar, *op. cit.*, II, letter #75, Serra to Bucareli, 2 July 1775.
[108] Bolton, *Palóu*, IV, p. 5.

through the entrance, until, as he states, he was "one league within the mouth and a quarter of a mile from the shore" when they were suddenly becalmed.[109] Then the current began to sweep the ship toward the mouth; Ayala however, ordered the main anchor dropped and it held in a sandy bottom at a depth of twenty-two fathoms.[110] The time was 10:30 on the night of August 5th.

Since the *San Carlos* was the first ship to enter the Bay, a certain interest attaches to the site of her first anchorage. Fortunately, the anchorage can be determined with considerable accuracy owing to facts recorded by Ayala in his log and from details drawn on the so-called Ayala "Plano del Puerto de San Francisco", dated 30 November 1775, which was prepared as a result of the explorations carried on during the next several weeks after the first night spent in the Bay.[111]

The Ayala *Plano* is the first carefully prepared chart and map of the San Francisco Bay area, compared with which the Costansó map is a mere fragment and the "Crespí" preparation a grave distortion. Cañizáres and Aguirre made careful soundings of the entire stretch of the Bay, all the way from some points outside of the Golden Gate into the farthest reaches of the southern estuary and the San Pablo and Suisun Bays lying to the north and east. Approximately 485 soundings are located in this chart, and can be counted. The soundings are indicated with numbers which refer to the depth in *brazas*, this measure being the Spanish fathom of about five and one-half feet. There are also eight anchor symbols shown, apparently to mark anchorages of the *San Carlos* and the launch or long-boat during the course of surveys made in the latter.

It happens that out of the some 485 sounding marks, one, and only one, is the number 22, and right next to it on the chart is an anchor symbol. The depth here indicated was perhaps not accurate.

---

[109] A Spanish *legua* was ca. 3.46 miles and a *milla* was ⅛ of a legua; hence, the ¼ milla mentioned put the *San Carlos* a little over a quarter of a mile offshore. This is stated in Spanish: " . . . 1 legua á dentro de la Boca y un quarto de milla de la Playa . . .". Cf. *Diario*, cited in note #115, below, and Appendix, the "Ayala" *Plano del Puerto de San Francisco*.

[110] Fathom is the translation of *braza* which is 2 *varas* or 1.6718 meters, or 5.46 feet.

[111] The Ayala log is known as the *Diario*, etc.; see note #115, below. The *Plano* was prepared by Cañizáres, but bears the name of the skipper; see note #113, below.

As noted, Captain Ayala ordered the anchor dropped at a time the ship was already being moved by an outgoing tide since way had been lost when the wind died, and it may be that the depth recorded was the result of a sounding taken at an angle. However, the use of the depth mark on the chart along with reference to that same depth of 22 brazas in the log, and the placement of the anchor symbol alongside the number, make it virtually certain that Pilot Cañizáres was thus marking the spot where the *San Carlos* was secured during the first hours inside the Bay; the spot was off present Sausalito.

It is also necessary to note that when Pilot Cañizáres returned to the *San Carlos* on the morning of the 6th of August at 6 A.M., he had come to the ship from the south side of the Bay where the day before he had found a safe anchorage. He had not been able to communicate this information to the captain because of inability to return to the ship; he explained to Captain Ayala, upon being questioned by the captain, that strong currents and the fatigue of his men had, despite two attempts, prevented him from reaching the ship. Thus, had the *San Carlos* sailed along the north shore of the Peninsula when she entered the Bay, instead of moving along the Marin coast, she would probably have found the launch, or the launch would have found her, on the evening of the 5th of August.

Finally, almost immediately after Cañizáres' return to the ship he was again sent out in the launch to explore an *ensenada* which Captain Ayala recorded as having a West-Northwest bearing from the position of the ship's anchorage. The Ayala *Plano* is equipped with a compass rose according to the North then observed, and when a parallel is drawn with the WNW direction, using the position of the number 22 anchorage as a starting point, the line touches the opening to Richardson Bay (called Carmelita Bay on the *Plano*) where Cañizáres found the bottom unsatisfactory for an anchorage owing to sticky mud (*fango pegajoso*).

Ayala next sought various anchorages on the north side of the Bay but finally moved his ship into the cove on Angel Island now called Hospital Cove, on the 13th of August. There the *San Carlos* remained safely at anchor until the 8th of September; in the meanwhile the Bay was charted by Cañizáres and the second pilot,

Juan Bautista Aguirre, using the ship's long-boat and on occasion the *cayuco*. The anchorage inside Fort Point, later to become well-known as the Presidio Anchorage, or the "Old Spanish Anchorage," was apparently never used by the *San Carlos*. However, there is considerable evidence that Cañizáres in his long-boat used that anchorage on the night of the 5th of August when he had been unable to return to the *San Carlos*.[112]

Captain Ayala left not only his log for the historical record, but also a brief, formal "Report of Don Juan Manuel de Ayala, Commander of the Packet Boat San Carlos to Don Antonio María Bucareli, Viceroy of New Spain on the Examination of the Port of San Francisco." This Report is a document of first importance to all readers interested in the beginnings of San Francisco. Here is the Captain's statement:

"Your Excellency: I have finished the orders under which I took command of the *San Carlos*, returning to this port of San Blas today, November 6th, after having visited the ports of Monterey and San Francisco.

"Although your Excellency will see in the account of my examination, together with the pilot, Don José Cañizáres' report of his examination and map he made of this port,[113] the nature of the work done, I will, notwithstanding, in this, give a brief account, that shows the port of San Francisco to be one of the best that I have seen on this coast from Cape Horn.

"After one hundred and one days of navigation, I arrived at the harbor of Monterey, where I had to remain till July 27th, discharging the cargo and making some repairs necessary for the safety of my vessel. On July 27th, I started in search of the Port of San Francisco, where I arrived on the night of August 5th. I remained there forty-four days, inspecting by myself, or by my pilot, with all possible accuracy, everything that pertains to this matter.

---

[112] There is an anchor symbol on the *Plano*, between Fort Point and Black Point (Fort Mason) with soundings of 7 and 8 brazas on either side of the symbol.

[113] It is obvious that the Ayala survey of the Bay would be more accurately described as the Cañizáres-Aguirre survey. The skipper's fairness in giving credit where credit is due is quite noteworthy.

"It is true that this port is good, not only for the beautiful harmony that offers to the view, but because it does not lack very good fresh water, wood, and ballast in abundance. Its climate though cold, is healthful and free from those troublesome fogs which we had daily in Monterey, because the fogs here hardly reach the entrance of the port, and once inside the harbor, the weather is very clear. To these many advantages is to be added the best: and this is that the heathen Indians around this port are so constant in their good friendship and so gentle in their manners, that I received them with pleasure on board several times, and I had the sailors frequently visit with them on land; so that from the first to the last day, they remained the same in their behaviour. This made me present them with trinkets, beads, and biscuit; the last they learned to ask for clearly in our language.

"There is no doubt that this good friendship was a great comfort to us, enabling us to make with less fear the reconnaissance that was ordered of me. Although in a letter written by Your Excellency to my predecessor, Don Miguel Manrique, dated January 2d, I read that it was possible we might find in San Francisco the land expedition undertaken by Captain Don Juan de Anza; I did not on that account refuse the offer of another small land expedition which the Captain of Monterey, Don Fernando de Rivera, made me. I did not see either of them while I remained in that port, but I did not, on that account, postpone the reconnaissance. I could not do all of this in person, because I was convalescing from a serious wound in my right foot, received April 3d by the accidental discharge of a double-barrel pistol, which Don Miguel Manrique had left loaded in the cabin. Notwithstanding this, I am satisfied that Don José Cañizáres executed with his usual ability everything I entrusted to his care. I therefore state to Your Excellency (in order that the merit of his work not be ignored), that as long as he was with me, he acted not only with his usual honesty, but showed such great talent in his profession that in the midst of my troubles I found him one to entrust with the more delicate points of my duty.

"On September 17th, I decided to leave the Port of San Francisco, as I considered the reconnaissance completed, and in doing this, having no wind, I was carried by the strong current against some rocks, injuring the rudder and breaking two female and one male bolts. This obliged me to enter a cove, where I repaired as well as possible the accident, and again tried to sail forth, a light breeze from the north (the only one I noticed in the forty-four days) aiding the sailing. On the 18th, because the rudder was injured, and those who had been on this coast before had warned me that at this time of year the weather was very severe, I determined to pass the Equinox at Monterey and arrived there on the 19th. At this port I found the frigate *Santiago*. The schooner came October 7th, and I left for San Blas on the 13th, where I am sick of my foot, but always desirous to obey Your Excellency.

"I pray the Lord to keep the life of Your Excellency many years.
"San Blas, November 9, 1775.
"Juan Manuel de Ayala.

"To His Excellency, Bailio Frey Don Antonio María Bucareli."[114]

Of the scores of details concerning the explorations of Ayala, Cañizáres, and Aguirre, reported in the writings of the two former, only a few need detain us. The most famous place names left by the expedition which have survived were *Isla de los Alcatrazes*, and *Isla de los Angeles*, which the present renderings of those names do not quite cover. No name was given by the explorers to the cove on Angel Island where the *San Carlos* lay at anchor; this cove is now known as Hospital Cove.

There seems little doubt that the name Isla de los Alcatrazes was intended to apply to today's Yerba Buena Island. When Cañizáres was sent out in the launch to search for a more central anchorage than the site off Sausalito, he apparently looked over not only Angel Island but also another island which Ayala described in his 12 August entry as "so barren and craggy that it could provide no shelter even for small craft and it was called the Alcatrazes because of the large numbers of them that were there."[115]

---

[114] Z. S. Eldredge, *et al.*, *The March of Portolá* . . . (including the Log of the San Carlos and Original Documents Translated and Annotated by E. J. Molera).

[115] Cf. Diario de la Navegacion que va á hacer el Teniente de Fragata de la Real

Later, also in the month of August, after Cañizáres had explored the northern reaches of the bay, he began his survey of the southern estuary. In the report of his reconnaissance Cañizáres states: "To the east [of Angel Island] lies another at a distance of two leagues which is craggy and steep without any shelter; it divides the mouth of the estuary [i.e., the southern estuary] into two channels through which the sea enters some twelve leagues."[116]

When Cañizáres prepared his chart of the Bay, which was under Ayala's cognizance and had to be approved by him, the presently-known Yerba Buena Island was given the name of *Y.ª de Alcatrazes*. This may be seen in the *Explicacion* drawn into the map. What is today known as Alcatraz Island was unnamed.[117]

Armada, y Capitan del Paquebot de S.M. nombrado Sn. Carlos, alias el Toison de Oro Dn. Juan Manuel de Ayala desde el Puerto de San. Blas situado en la Latitud de 21°, 22 mis. y en la Longd. Oriental del Meridiano de Tenerife 271°, 8 ms. al Presidio de Monterrey, y descubierta del Puerto de Sn. Franco. formando el primer Meridiano en dho. Puerto de Sn. Blas oy 19 de Marzo del Año de 1775. Microfilm, *Bancroft Library*. The Spanish description of the "other island": ". . . tan arida y escarpada que ni para lanchas havia puerto â esta le puse de los Alcatrazes por la abundancia que tiene de ellos . . ."

[116] (Ynforme del reconocimto.) ye descripcion del nuevo Puerto de S. Franco., situado por una prudente congetura en la latitud N. de 37 grs. 53 ms. y en la longitud occidental del meridiano de San Blas 17 grs. 10'. Microfilm, *Bancroft Library*. The statement of Cañizáres, in Spanish, follows: "Al leste de esta Isla [i.e., Angel Island] se halla à distancia de ella dos leguas otra aspera escabrosa y de ningun resguardo, la qual divide la voca del estero en dos cañones por donde se introduce el mar como doze leguas . . ."

[117] See Appendix, pp. 135-136, for reproduction of Ayala map. Z. S. Eldredge, *The Beginnings of San Francisco*, I, 45-51, believes that Alcatraz was named when Cañizáres searched for a better anchorage than the spot off present-day Sausalito; his exploration was made in the ship's launch. Later, thinks Eldredge, the "other island" [present Yerba Buena] was explored. Then, when the map was prepared. Cañizáres, according to the Eldredge view, made an incorrect identification of the islands on the map he had himself prepared.

However, in differing from the Eldredge interpretation, it can be pointed out that the language of Ayala and Cañizáres is strikingly similar in the description provided of the appearance of the island and its unsuitability as an anchorage (probably because of what Cañizáres wrote and said); that both men were involved in the preparation of the map—Cañizáres drew it and Ayala as expedition commander had to take responsibility for it. Moreover, the navigator's view of Yerba Buena (which it is being maintained here was Cañizáres' *Alcatraz*) is that it *does* divide the estuary into two channels; and this cannot be said of the island today called Alcatraz.

The first known map which shows the present names of the *three* islands referred to here is the one of Frederick William Beechey in 1826. See Neil Harlow, "The Maps of San Francisco Bay and the Town of Yerba Buena to One Hundred Years Ago", *Pacific Historical Review*, XVI, #4 (November, 1947). Mr. Harlow points out, p. 372,

Of religious significance, and illustrative of the spirit of those times, on the day the *San Carlos* commenced her voyage from Monterey a Novena was begun to "our Seraphic Father San Francisco," and on the ninth day, at its conclusion, the ship arrived "at the desired port."[118] After some days had been spent in the port and when things were going quite well, on August 27th a mass of thanksgiving was said on the shore of the *Isla de los Angeles* (in "Hospital Cove") and, as the Spanish flag raised, nine shouts of "Viva el Rey" were given.[119]

"Yerba Buena Island was so named by the expedition, the label 'Los Alcatraces' having been transferred to present-day Alcatraz Island."

However, Beechey was not the first to modify the Ayala-Cañizáres names for the *two* principal islands. In 1794 there appeared a chart known as the "Chart of the Port of San Francisco and the Battery of San Joaquin." [Reproduction in Irving Berdine Richman, *California Under Spain and Mexico, 1535–1847, etc.* (1911), following p. 344. Richman provides no citation for his access to the map. See microfilm, Bancroft Library, *AGN*, Californias, V. 47, #8, for letter of Governor Diego de Borica, 1 January 1795 to the Viceroy, stating that the said Chart is being sent by ordinary mail to Mexico. Unfortunately, the chart, which is described as being of large size and in color, is not found in the Bancroft microfilm, though cited in the Bolton *Guide*, pp. 160–161. A photostat copy is supposed to be in the Pomona College Library, according to Harlow, *The Maps of San Francsico Bay, etc.* (1950).]

The *Fuerte de San Joaquin*, and this is stated on the chart, had been constructed by the "Governador interno de la Peninsula de Californias, D. Jose Joaquin de Arrillaga" on the orders of the Viceroy, the Conde de Revilla Gigedo. The fort was located at the top of the *Cantil Blanco* (theWhite Cliff, today's Fort Point, much modified from the sheer natural wonder it must have been). See Father Font's description, above, pp. 79–80, text, where Anza had indicated a battery should be built during his 1776 survey. The anchorage below the indicated site of the Presidio is referred to as the "old anchorage" (*Fondo antiguo*), and a dotted line leads through the Gate to an anchor symbol located opposite a position marked P.to dla. Yervabuena. The dotted line is labelled "Entrance to San Francisco to the new anchorage."

Offshore from this Yervabuena is an island named "Y.ª de los Angeles" (present Yerba Buena Island), and the *Y.ª de Alcatrazes* on this chart is obviously located where present Alcatraz is known to be. The bulk of present Angel Island and the shoreline of Tiburon and Belvedere are partly, not completely, outlined, but Angel is unnamed.

This chart presents evidence of major error committed by the Spaniards themselves with reference to the three islands, and perhaps also about the anchorages, since the Yerba Buena anchorage was not used before about 1824, according to the later testimony of Port Captain W. A. Richardson, though Vancouver had probably used it in November, 1792 until he was requested to move his vessel under the Presidio at the "old anchorage". For a very detailed and carefully documented discussion of aspects of this anchorage question, see J. N. Bowman, "The Spanish Anchorage in San Francisco Bay", *CHSQ*, XXV, #4, (Dec., 1946).

Beechey's error in the naming of the three major islands probably has some explanation not yet understood.

[118] Bolton, *Palóu*, IV.

[119] From Ayala's *Diario*, entry for August 28. The entry reads: "Se dixo una misa

Captain Ayala had maintained a program of vigilance in expectation of the arrival of the supporting land-party, and even, possibly, of Anza himself. Certainly twice, and possibly three times, parties were sent out to seek the land expeditions. On August 21st, in the ship's launch or long-boat, and on August 31st in the *cayuco*, second pilot Aguirre proceeded to the harbor's mouth; and on the 14th of September both pilots were sent to the harbor entrance by Captain Ayala to observe the time of low tide. On two of these trips the parties went ashore and visited the site of the cross at Pt. Lobos, and it may be that the ship's chaplain, Father Vicente de Santa María, was a member of these visits. Regrettably for the completion of the plans earlier made in Monterey, the local land party did not arrive before the departure of the *San Carlos* for Monterey, and Anza, of course, at that time had not even left Sonora.

Father Palóu tells about the land expedition from Monterey that had been expected to rendezvous with Ayala and which arrived on the 22nd (of September) "at the beach of the Gulf of the Farallones." The party included Father Palóu, Fray Miguel de la Campa Cos, chaplain of the frigate *Santiago*, and the ship's Commander, Don Bruno Eceta, with some members of the crew and nine soldiers. On the beach, wrote Palóu, "we found the *cayuco* which was built on Carmelo River, full of water and sand, and not far off the oars. We followed the beach as far as the high hill at the mouth of the harbor, which we ascended, and at the foot of the cross I found two letters written by Father Fray Vicente Santa María.

"In the first letter he informed me of their safe arrival at the harbor, and the ease with which they had entered at night and dropped anchor.[120] In the second he told me that the expedition had landed, and that the exploration was now concluded satisfactorily,

de Gracias en la Playa de la Isle de los Angeles è Yzando la Vandera Española se dieron nuebe vozes de Viva el Rey." In the opinion of this writer it is regrettable that the scene of thanksgiving which took place in the sheltered cove of Angel Island has not received historical recognition through some ceremony which would fix the name of the cove as "Ayala Cove", instead of "Hospital Cove" which is its present designation.

[120] Captain Ayala had experienced no such sense of security during the entry.

9

The Selection of Sites for the Presidio and the Mission: March, 1776

About a week earlier, in far-off Horcasitas, Sonora, the Second Anza Expedition had begun its march. By January, 1776, the party reached San Gabriel mission, but here a stop was made while Anza with Father Font accompanied Commandant Rivera to San Diego. Mission San Diego de Alcalá had been the scene of an Indian uprising (the night of November 4, 1775) when Father Luis Jayme, a carpenter, and a blacksmith, all of them Spaniards, were killed by the attackers. Rivera was traveling south to mete out punishment to the guilty. It was during this time that the antagonism of Rivera toward the San Francisco enterprise became overtly apparent, but it is quite difficult to evaluate Rivera's attitude. Personal jealousy and personality differences between Rivera and Anza are certainly apparent as one considers the two leaders. Rivera, as an experienced explorer, had sincere convictions that Anza's program was not well conceived.

Rivera first tried to talk Anza out of completing his mission. Later, when talk had failed, he found various ways to be uncooperative. Father Pedro Font, the diarist and observer for the expedition, attributed Rivera's attitude to the latter's fear that Anza and Font would make a better exploration than had Rivera, and would provide the Viceroy with a report in conflict with the one Rivera himself had made. Font quoted Rivera as saying repeatedly: "Why do you want to go there and tire yourselves out, when I have already told you that I have carefully examined all that region, and have reported to the Viceroy that there is nothing there for the purpose in mind?"[122]

Father Font even suggested that at one point in the discussions "Señor Anza was somewhat inclined to go no further [a conclusion most difficult to believe], and so we were always talking about the matter, asking Señor Ribera various questions as to what he knew and had seen, and insisting on the continuation of the journey."

Font also reports that "Señor Anza still insisted that the people should go to the port of San Francisco, saying that the viceroy had urgently charged him with this, and had told him that if no suitable place were found near the mouth of the port, the settlement should be made wherever he might think best, even though it might be some leagues from the port, in order that thereby it might be seen that the harbor already had been occupied on the part of Spain.[123]

"Señor Ribera replied that this was a very different matter, for he had been ordered that the settlement should be established near the port, and for this reason he had reported that this could not be, because there was no good site there; but that he would not

---

[122] Bolton, *Anza*, IV. "Font's Complete Diary of the Second Anza Expedition." The discussions with Rivera are recorded in the very long entry for 7 February 1776, made in San Diego.

Earlier, in 1775, Rivera had also received a letter from Sergeant Ortega, dated 5 May, San Diego, after Ortega had heard the news that Anza would come to California with a colonizing expedition. Ortega reported to his friend and superior officer that the expedition was to establish a presidio at the Port of San Francisco and also a mission, or missions, and then added the thoughts that this enterprise would not be able to reach the port without launches; that it was an undertaking of considerable moment, and would need God's help to be successful. Ortega's letter is an additional item in the list of items bearing on the confusion which even to this time still existed concerning the Port of San Francisco, and the "estuary". It can hardly be doubted from Ortega's words that he considered the Anza expedition to have a different goal from the one which it ultimately reached. Also it is clear that Ortega, one of the discoverers of San Francisco Bay, still did not understand that he had, in fact, made a discovery. [For the Ortega item, see *Arch. of Calif. Prov. St. Papers*, 162 ff., Ms, Bancroft Library. This item was used by Brown, see note #87, above, though the present writer does not agree with Brown's comment that "Ortega wrote to *warn* Rivera that Anza was said to be on the way . . . " (italics, T.E.T.).]

[123] This interpretation of the charge to Anza could be reconciled with the views of Palóu and Rivera concerning the suitability of the San Francisquito [Palo Alto] site for a mission; text, pp. 58 and 62, Spanish theory with respect to ownership is discussed in Henry R. Wagner, "Creation of Rights of Sovereignty Through Symbolic Acts", *Pacific Historical Review*, VII, #4 (December, 1938).

deny that places might be found at a distance from it, and this being the case he felt very much better. Finally, seeing that Señor Anza was determined to go to examine the port, and that he could not prevent us, Señor Ribera concluded by saying: 'Well, friend, go ahead, go ahead, and explore to your satisfaction and do what to you seems best. On the return you will tell me what you have seen, and from this moment [I will] agree to whatever you may decide.'

"From that night Señor Anza was very much offended at Señor Ribera because he was so hostile to the new establishment; and this decision of Señor Anza, with whom I, as his companion, made myself a participant in the hatred of Señor Ribera, was the beginning of the tilts and encounters which we had afterward . . ."[124]

The truth was that Fate had passed Rivera by. He had been resentful of the Anza exploration and discovery of the land route from Sonora to Alta California which he, Rivera, had claimed to have thought about himself; he had made his exploration with Father Palóu and had filed a report with the Viceroy which named only one possible mission site on the peninsula; and now Anza had appeared with colonists and armed with clear instructions to further explore and then to occupy the port of San Francisco. The "tilts and encounters" referred to by Father Font between these two frontier captains resulted in robbing Anza of the honor of a direct participation in the founding of the Royal Presidio of San Francisco and Mission San Francisco de Asís.

The entire membership of the second Anza expedition, people and livestock, reached Monterey in March, 1776, and Father Font points out that there was a discontent amongst the colonists as there was with the missionaries at the prospect of further delay in reaching San Francisco's port. "And the four fathers, who had been here for two years, and found themselves here as if on deposit, being destined for the two missions which were to be founded there, were now tired of waiting any longer," reports Font.

On Wednesday, March 13, Anza, though ill, wrote a letter to

---

[124] Bolton, *Anza*, IV. Font's *Complete Diary*, entry for 7 February 1776, concluded.

Commandant Rivera, a letter he showed to Father Font. "In it he [Anza] told him [Rivera] that he was going to examine the port of San Francisco, and, in case he found a good site he offered on his return to go there to escort the people, if Señor Ribera agreed, even though for this purpose he might have to remain a month longer. He exhorted Ribera to agree to this plan, because the viceroy would be greatly pleased to have that port occupied immediately, and to have it effected by establishing the people there. He added that the people also wished to go there because that was their destination, and that they were discontented in Monterey because of the discomfort in which they found themselves; and finally, that unless this should be done promptly the fathers were determined to leave on the first bark which might come, because they did not wish to wait any longer. It was this letter which caused Señor Ribera such hostility to Señor Ansa, because he had declared himself on the side of the fathers and in favor of that establishment, to which Señor Ribera himself was so much opposed."

Anza remained somewhat under the weather during the next few days, but on Sunday March 17 Father Font recorded in his diary that the commander was "somewhat better this morning." Also on that day the message was despatched to Commander Rivera, previously written, with the additional note that Anza hoped a reply would be forthcoming by the time the reconnaissance of the port was completed. On the afternoon of the 22nd Anza, Font and other members of the exploring party journeyed from the mission to the presidio of Monterey, and on Saturday, March 23rd the expedition started, with its purpose being, according to Font's entry, "to explore the port of San Francisco, the Rio Grande [Father Crespí's expression], and the sites suitable for the two missions and the fort or settlement . . .

"We left the presidio of Monterey at half past nine in the morning, Commander Ansa, I, the lieutenant [Joseph Joaquín Moraga], and eleven soldiers (eight from Tubac, two from Monterey who went on the journey with Captain Fages, and the corporal from there called Robles [Juan José], who went on the journey with Captain Ribera), the last three going in order that as experienced men they might guide us to the port and river. There were also the necessary muleteers and servants, six in number, making altogether twenty persons."

On the fifth day after leaving Monterey camp was made (Wednesday, March 27) on the banks "of a lake or spring of very fine water near the mouth of the port of San Francisco" (Mountain Lake) and then Anza, Font, Moraga and four soldiers visited the site of the cross which had been set up by Captain Rivera and Father Palóu in December 1774. They found the cross lying on the ground, "and now without the form of a cross, perhaps because the Indians took from it the rope with which it was tied and held in shape." Father Font spent some time in mapping, using a "graphometer", and then the party went to the beach (below Pt. Lobos and Seal Rocks) to see the *cayuco* which was now broken in pieces. Anza secured two of its fragments.

"We again ascended the sand hills, descended to the arroyo, and crossed high hills until we reached the edge of the white cliff which forms the end of the mouth of the port, and where begins the great estuary containing islands. The cliff is very high and perpendicular, so that from it one can spit into the sea. From here we saw the pushing and resistance which the out-going water of the estuary makes against that of the sea, forming there a sort of ridge like a wave in the middle, and it seems as if a current is visible. We saw the spouting of whales, a shoal of dolphins or tunny fish, sea otter, and sea lions. On this elevation the commander decided to erect a cross, ordering it made at once so that he might set it up the next day." Then they returned to their camp.

"This place," wrote Father Font, "and its vicinity has abundant pasturage, plenty of firewood, and fine water, all good advantages for establishing here the presidio or fort which is planned. It lacks timber, for there is not a tree on all those hills, though the oaks and other trees along the road are not very far away. The soldiers chased some deer, of which we saw many today, but got none of them. We also found antlers of the large elk which are so very plentiful on the other side of the estuary. The sea is so quiet in the harbor that the waves scarcely break and from the camp site one hardly heard them, although it was so near. Here and near the lake there are *yerba buena* and so many lilies that I had them almost inside my tent."

Font mentions Indians who came to their camp and brought them firewood; Anza gave them glass beads as reward and they departed. Also provided by Father Font is his sense of wonder at the beauty of the Bay. To him it appeared as "a marvel of nature . . . the harbor of harbors, because of its great capacity, and of several small bays which it enfolds in its margins or beach and in its islands." The entry for Wednesday also mentions a minor altercation between Font and Anza about the purposes of the expedition.

"As soon as we returned from the reconnaissance I said to Señor Ansa: 'Señor, now that you wish to erect a cross at the port tomorrow, order it made right off, so that in the morning after Mass I may bless it, if you think well, before going to erect it.' . . . He replied: 'All right, that shall be done, Father.' Then, turning his back to me, he went into his tent, snorting and saying between his teeth: 'You always come with "if you think it well, if you think it well!"'' The fact is that he could not bear to have me give my opinion about anything."

Also Font reports that he began to read from the diaries of Crespí and Palóu, and that Anza would not listen to him, but got up and walked away. Font followed him, saying that Anza had moved in order not to listen, and that he was only using the diary "because we came to explore the port and the good sites for the two missions" and that the diary might serve to afford them much light.

Anza replied that he did not need the diary, that if any doubt arose in his mind he would ask about it. "He said that it was not his duty to seek sites for the missions, for this task belonged to Señor Ribera; that his duty was solely to explore the port in order to establish the presidio on it; that he would take care to fulfill his obligation and be guided by what might seem best to him, according to how the country might appear, etc. . . . We talked a little while, very familiarly and in a friendly way, but he appeared somewhat hurt because I had touched upon a subject which was his affair, for he could not bear that I should give him my opinion about anything.

"I note this down in order to show the tact with which it is necessary to conduct oneself with persons of sensitive nature and satisfied with themselves." Father Font says that he and Anza got along well after that, again became harmonious, "on account of the care with which he desired to make and did make the exploration of the port and river, and because of the tilts with Señor Ribera which took place when we returned. We continued in friendly harmony until we finished the journey, when I again fell out of his good graces, because he did not need me any more or because up to that time he had concealed his dislike."

On Thursday, March 28 Font made the important entry which tells of the fixing of the fort site, and on this day he also revealed within himself a remarkable gift of prophecy. "I said Mass. In the morning the weather was fair, although there were some clouds which scarcely permitted me to observe; but at length by dint of care and patience I succeeded in making the observation. The commander decided to erect the holy cross, which I blessed after Mass, on the extreme point of the white cliff at the inner terminus of the mouth of the port. At eight o'clock in the morning he and I went there with the lieutenant and four soldiers, and the cross was erected on a place high enough so that it could be seen from all the entry of the port and from a long distance away, and at the foot of it the commander left written on a paper under some stones a notice of his coming and of his exploration of this port.[125]

---

[125] Father Font's *Complete Diary* has been used as containing more detail and descriptive information than does Anza's. For the entry on Thursday, March 28, Anza provides the additional information that "I went to the narrowest opening made by the mouth of the port, *where nobody had been before* [italics, T.E.T.]. There I set up a cross, at its foot I buried under the ground a notice of what I have seen, in order that it may serve as a guide to any vessels that may enter, as well as a report of what I am going on to explore in order to establish the fort belonging to this harbor . . . " Anza's *Diary* is found in Bolton, *Anza,* III. The complete title of the Diary is instructive: "Diary of the March and Explorations Which I, the Undersigned Lieutenant-Colonel and Captain of the Royal Presidio of Tubac in the Province and Government of Sonora, Am Making a Second Time from the Foregoing Province to Northern California. By order of the most excellent Señor Baylio Frey Don Antonio María Bucareli y Ursúa, Viceroy, Governor, and Captain-General of New Spain, as is shown by his superior decree of the 24th November of the past year of 1774, for the purpose of escorting thirty soldiers with their commander and sergeant to the California named, for the reinforcement of the royal presidio of San Carlos de Monte Rey, and for the establishment of the port of San Francisco, all married and all recruited in the province named, and whose women and children and other dependents

"On leaving we ascended a small hill and then entered upon a mesa that was very green and flower-covered, with an abundance of wild violets. The mesa is very open, of considerable extent, and level, sloping a little toward the harbor. It must be about half a league wide and somewhat longer, getting narrower until it ends right at the white cliff. This mesa affords a most delightful view, for from it one sees a large part of the port and its islands, as far as the other side, the mouth of the harbor, and of the sea all that the sight can take in as far as beyond the farallones. Indeed, although in my travels I saw very good sites and beautiful country, I saw none which pleased me so much as this. And I think that if it could be well settled like Europe there would not be anything more beautiful in all the world, for it has the best advantages for founding in it a most beautiful city, which all the conveniences desired, by land as well as by sea, with that harbor so remarkable and so spacious, in which may be established shipyards, docks, and anything that might be wished.

"This mesa the commander selected as the site for the new settlement and fort which were to be established on this harbor; for, being on a height, it is so commanding that with muskets it can defend the entrance to the mouth of the harbor, while a gunshot away it has water to supply the people, namely, the spring or lake where we halted."[126]

After the ceremony of erecting the cross was completed Captain Anza decided to continue his exploration "for he had decided not to return until he had finished seeing all the advantages of this site and its environs, even though he might spend the entire day at it." Father Font was sent back to camp "in order not to miss the observation" and Anza evidently followed more or less along the shoreline toward the east, returning to camp himself by five o'clock "very well pleased." He had found plentiful timber and firewood, much water in several springs or lakes, abundant lands for raising crops, and finally, a vast supply of pasturage in all the country, "so

are set forth more at length below, together with the total number of those going upon this expedition."

[126] The mesa described by Father Font runs from Fort Point toward Mountain Lake, well above and west of the Presidio parade grounds and Officers Club. Part of this mesa is occupied by the Presidio Golf Course. Bolton refers to this as the "table land, south of Ft. Point, occupied by the Presidio grounds".

that the new settlement will be able to have plentiful fuel, water, and grass or pasturage for the horses, all near by." It was agreed, however, that the immediate vicinity lacked timber for large buildings, although for huts and barracks and for the stockade of the presidio there were plenty of trees in the groves. But heavier timber could be secured from the *Llano de los Robles*,[127] so-called because of the thick growth of oak trees, and from the stands of cedars "and other trees" on the high ranges to the south.

The expedition broke camp on Friday March 29, sending the pack train by a direct route to the San Mateo arroyo but themselves traveling about a league to the east, one to the east-southeast, and one to the southeast.[128] "Passing through wooded hills and over flats with good lands, in which we encountered two lagoons and some springs of good water, with plentiful grass, fennel, and other useful herbs, we arrived at a beautiful arroyo which, because it was Friday of Sorrows, we called the *Arroyo de los Dolores*. On its banks we found much and very fragrant manzanita and other plants, and many wild violets. Near it the lieutenant planted a little maize and chickpeas to test the soil, which to us appeared very good, and I concluded that this place was very pretty and the best for the establishment of one of the two missions. It appeared to me that the other might be founded at the arroyo of San Mateo, so that in this way they would have the two missions near the port, as it was desired, and to this opinion of mine the fathers were inclined.

"We went a little further, and from a small elevation there I

---

[127] Identified by H. E. Bolton as beginning on the other side of Calabasas Creek. See Appendix, the "Crespí" Map.

[128] Anza's entry for Friday, March 29, contains two very obvious slaps at Rivera although Anza seems to be writing somewhat generally. One item reads: " . . . but the exploration that has been made on this occasion, *in the region where it was prognosticated that there would be the same sterility as at the west of our port mentioned*, shows that this region, with the exception of what relates to timber for large beams, is not only fertile but extremely so."

He continues then, with: "Therefore, this presidio and fort will have an abundance and variety of water, firewood, and building stone. It will not lack a place in which to plant good fields, although somewhat distant, nor pastures for cattle without equal in quality and abundance. And besides enjoying these fine advantages, *of which those who have formerly come as far as the mouth of the port have not even had hopes*, it will enjoy even more if established at the place already mentioned, where it is narrowest, to mark which I am leaving erected a cross, as I indicated on the 28th . . . " [italics, T.E.T.].

observed the trend of the port in this direction. I saw that its extremity was toward the east-southeast, and that a very high redwood [the *palo alto*] which stands on the bank of the arroyo of San Francisco, visible from a long distance, rising like a great tower in the Llano de los Robles, and whose height I afterward measured, lay to the southeast. Near this elevation, at the end of the hill on the side toward the port, there is a good piece of level land dominated by the Arroyo de los Dolores. This arroyo enters the plain by a fall which it makes on emerging from the hills, and with it everything can be irrigated, and at the same fall a mill can be erected, for it is very suitable for this purpose."[129]

The expedition then left the site of the future mission San Francisco de Asís, which Father Font evidently selected and where Lieutenant Moraga planted the first seeds, and continued their exploration. This took them around the southern arm of the Bay, through the *contra costa*, and to the Carquinez Straits area. The expedition returned to Monterey on April 8.

Father Serra[130] and Father Font[131] both mention that Rivera had not responded to the message which Anza had sent to him on the 17th of March. Anza now decided to leave Monterey. Under better circumstances he would have secured the cooperation of Rivera and might have participated directly in the establishment of the Royal Presidio and possibly also the mission. Anza believed that he had followed his instructions to the letter. He had been ordered to recruit soldiers for the expedition; to lead them to Monterey; to deliver them to the commander "of those establishments"; to assist in the exploration of the "River of San Francisco", so as to be able to report on his findings; and to return by the same route used to his own presidio.[132] Father Serra in writing about Anza immedi-

---

[129] Bolton, *Anza*, IV. Font, *Complete Diary*, entry for 29 March.

[130] Tibesar, *op. cit.*, #99.

[131] Font, *Complete Diary*, entry for April 12.

[132] Viceroy Bucareli later expressed considerable irritation at the fact that Rivera and Anza had not been able to cooperate according to his orders. In a letter to Gálvez, Mexico August 27, 1776, Bucareli pointed out that "The Commission of Don Juan Bautista de Anza was directed principally to the establishment of the presidio projected for the port of San Francisco with two missions in the neighborhood designed to attract the heathen Indians who lived there. . . . " Bolton, *Anza*, V. See also text, pp. 96–98.

ately after the San Francisco Bay exploration as much as says that Anza seemed quite well satisfied with what he had accomplished.[133] The Viceroy, as appears later, had fully expected more than exploration.

Although Serra had exhibited irritation at Anza's insistence on eating well, and had complained about the drain on mission supplies occasioned by the arrival of the colonists, the Father President was all in all highly appreciative of the Anza-Font explorations. For the first time Serra accepted the difference between Cabrera's "port of San Francisco" and the new discovery, and he acknowledged this in his letter to Viceroy Bucareli, written in the latter part of June, 1776. " . . . The facts, Most Excellent Lord, are as Your Excellency had thought, and all my misgivings have been dispelled in the presence of the realities of the place—its ample provision for disembarking. *It is indeed the true Harbor of St. Francis,* and will be settled when the fort is established in the place selected for it by Lieutenant Colonel Don Juan Bautista de Anza.[134] It is called *El Cantil Blanco.* After that the mission is to be founded as near to it as circumstances will allow. This is the mission that had been planned before, and its name is to be San Francisco Mission. And so no bells are needed, nor furnishings,

---

[133] Tibesar, *ibid.* In this letter, 13 April 1776, Father Serra, as stated, reported Anza's satisfaction with what he himself had accomplished despite Anza's discontent with Rivera's "delay and inactivity." When Anza's own sense of his having fulfilled his commission is related to Viceroy Bucareli's expression of disappointment about the San Franciso program there is room left for speculation concerning the precise meaning of the commission itself. Did Anza give up too quickly because of his differences with Rivera? Was he forced to conclude that only his disappearance from the scene would allow Rivera to act? Anza left Monterey on 14 April 1776. It was not until 8 May that Rivera, in San Diego, sent an order to Moraga for the founding of the Presidio, but not yet of the Mission.

Font, *Complete Diary,* entry for April 12, also reports, relative to Anza's eating habits, that the fathers were generous at Monterey and "put up many vegetables for us for the journey, such as cauliflower, lettuce, and tender beans, and also a great quantity of dried salmon. But I never tasted of any, nor did I see it again, because Señor Anza kept it all in order to use it for his own satisfaction."

[134] Italics, T.E.T. This statement on the part of Father Serra seems to be a confirmation of his idea that there had to be a "true" harbor of San Francisco. Serra had never, up to the time of this letter, accepted the new discovery as anything but a barrier to the "true" port of San Francisco. The Viceroy's references to Serra as a man who "knows the country" or who "knows the regions" was simply an article of faith with him, and is not borne out by the facts of Serra's understanding of the significance of the inner Bay of San Francisco.

nor livestock, because it has been provided with all such neces-
saries long ago, and the Fathers appointed to this foundation have
already been placed in possession of them. I have already sent in
their names to Your Excellency."[135]

In the same letter Father Serra revealed his understanding of
how Commandant Rivera's reluctance to support the mission
foundation could be taken in stride through the force of circumstances. "When the said desired missions will be founded, with
all that has occurred recently", he wrote, "I confess that I am
unable to give any answer. The latest news that I can supply in
this regard, and I now forward it to Your Excellency, is that, on
the seventeenth of this month, the Lieutenant Don Joseph Joachim
Moraga started from this Presidio of Monterey with a number of
families with him—both small and large—together with the livestock—mares and mules—community property, or that belonging
to particular individuals, for the foundation of the fort, in the
aforesaid place, where they said they would arrive in seven days.
According to that, the foundation may take place on the Feast of
Saint John the Baptist. Although the permission that the Commandant gave for the said foundation, at the request of Señor
Anza, did not include any mission, I did not make any comment
about it. The way I felt was that the two religious who are to
found the first and nearest mission should go with the company
and take with them the cattle, which amounts to more than ninety
head. The mules too that I could spare them should go, and a
number of quintals of hardtack which Don Bruno Hezeta had left
to me for the purpose, and groceries as well, Indian boys, bells,
furnishings, farm tools, etc. What could not go by land was put
on the boat, ready to sail for the same destination. [The *San
Carlos* had arrived at Monterey on June 3rd.]

"All of this they already have in their possession; and when
permission is given them, all they will have to do is move it some
few leagues, more or less, and begin setting up a mission. Don
Fernando Quirós, Captain of the boat, had the courtesy to give me
a promise that if the mission were to be started, he would take it

---

[135] Tibesar, *op. cit.*, III, #102, Monterey, June 27, 1776.

upon himself, with the help of the sailors, to provide the Fathers with a house, a church and a granary; but if they were not to begin it, they would build the fort, the church and residence for the Fathers.

"With the enthusiasm and the contentment of mind with which they all set out, I expect that the new pueblo will be well worth seeing before long. I already feel overjoyed to be able to offer Your Excellency my sincere congratulations on something we both have had close at heart for many a long day. May your Excellency live a thousand years to accomplish as great, or even greater things, which lead so much to the glory of God!"[136]

---

[136] Virtually the same information and commentary provided the Viceroy by Serra was also included in a letter to the Guardian, dated at San Diego October 7, 1776, where Serra had arrived on July 11, after a twelve-day voyage aboard *El Príncipe* which had left Monterey on 29 June. Serra had also provided the name for the "second mission," namely, *Santa Clara*. The site for Santa Clara was originally placed a day's journey east of San Buenaventura Mission, near present Castaic. Serra considered it unlikely that the original site would be used; hence, his practical solution was simply to transfer the name to the north and use the items in readiness for Santa Clara at the new site. As he said: "If we arrange it this way, we would not have to take the clothes off one saint, to dress up the other." Tibesar, *op. cit.*, III, items #102 and 106; and II, p. 473, note #73.

10

The Founding of the Presidio and the Mission: September and October, 1776

Father Palóu tells that "On the 17th day of June, 1776, about two in the afternoon, the company of soldiers and families from Sonora set out from Monterey. It was composed of its commander, Lieutenant Don José Joaquín Moraga, a sergeant, two corporals, and ten soldiers, all with their wives and families except the commander, who had left his in Sonora.[137] In addition there were seven families of settlers, rationed and provisioned by the king; other persons attached to the soldiers and their families; five servant boys, muleteers and vaqueros, who conducted about two hundred of the king's cattle and some belonging to individuals, and the mule train which carried the provisions and utensils necessary for the road. All of the foregoing belonged to the new presidio. And for whatever concerned the first mission that was to be founded, we two ministers, Father Fray Pedro Benito Cambón and I, went with two servants who conducted the loads, and three unmarried Indian neophytes, two of them from Old California and the other from the mission of Carmelo, who drove the cattle for the mission, numbering eighty-six, which were incorporated with those for the presidio.

"The officers of the vessels, with their pilots and chaplains, wished to accompany the expedition, and they all did so for about

---

[137] Moraga's account of the founding expedition states that he "set the troops in motion" and accompanied the expedition for about half a league from the presidio and then returned to assist in loading provisions aboard the *San Carlos*. He overtook the party on the morning of the 19th, at 2 a.m., at their encampment.

half a league. From this point the captain of the *Príncipe* and all the pilots turned back; but Don Fernando Quirós continued for the first day's march with the two father chaplains as far as the Monterey River, where the expedition halted and camped. On the following day, after having watched all the people cross the river and seen the line formed on that broad plain by all those people, the pack trains, cattle, and the horse herd, they returned to Monterey after taking farewell in the hope that we would soon meet in the port of Our Father San Francisco.

"The expedition continued by the same road which was traveled in the exploration of that harbor in the year 1774, . . . But the day's marches were shorter, in order not to fatigue the little children and the women, especially those who were pregnant, and for this reason it was even necessary to make several stops. On the whole way there was not a single mishap, thanks to God. . . .

"On the 27th day of June the expedition arrived in the neighborhood of the harbor, and the commander ordered the camp halted on the bank of a lagoon called by Señor Anza Nuestra Señora de los Dolores, which is in sight of the bay of Los Llorones and the beach of the bay or arm of the sea which runs to the southeast, with the intention of waiting here for the bark in order to select the spot for the founding of the fort and presidio, and in the meantime to explore the land.[138] On the following day he ordered a shelter of

---

[138] Moraga states: "On the 27th at half past six in the morning I set out with the soldiers from the site of San Mateo, and at half past eleven, without any incident, we camped at the port of San Francisco and the Laguna de los Dolores. This very day I gave orders to the sergeant to set the soldiers at cutting trees for the building of their houses, an occupation which they continued daily, so that when the vessel should arrive everything would be prepared, and when on consultation with Don Fernando Quirós we should decide on the most suitable site for the presidio we should be ready to go at once to cut timber for its erection." The account being followed is taken from Chapters XVIII to XXII inclusive in Palóu, *Historical Memoirs*, IV. Father Palóu in his *Life of Fray Junípero Serra*, Maynard J. Geiger, ed. (1955), provides a slightly different version from the one in the *Historical Memoirs*. There is added, for instance, a bit of detail about the first encampment. The printed Spanish form of Palóu's *Life of Serra* [*Relación Histórica de la Vida y Apostólicas Tareas del Venerable Padre Fray Junípero Serra* (Mexico, 1787)] tells us that on the 27th day of June [the expedition] arrived in the vicinity of the Port and made camp with fifteen army tents on the banks of a large lagoon which emptied into the arm of the sea of the port. [Dia 27 de Junio llegamos á la cercania de este Puerto, y se formó el Real de 15 Tiendas de Campaña á la orilla de una grande Laguna que vacía en el brazo de mar del Puerto . . .]

In the *California Historical Society Quarterly*, XIV, #2 (June, 1935) may be found an

branches built to serve as a chapel in which to celebrate the holy
sacrifice of the Mass. In it the first Mass was said on the 29th, the
feast of the great, holy apostles, San Pedro and San Pablo, and we
continued to celebrate in it every day until the camp was moved to
the site which it occupies near the landing place, when the ground
and the convenience of water permitted it."

The site of the future San Francisco mission remained as their
camp site for almost exactly one month. In Father Palóu's words:
"For an entire month the expedition remained in that camp, which
was composed of field tents, waiting for the bark. Meanwhile
soldiers, citizens, and servants employed themselves in cutting logs
in order to have this much done when the bark should arrive. The
lieutenant busied himself in exploring the land in the vicinity,
where he found some springs of water, lagoons, pastures, and good
sites for all kinds of stock. Near the white cliff he found two
springs of water sufficient for the use of the presidio, and not far
from them he found a good plain which is in sight of the harbor
and entrance, and also of its interior. As soon as he saw the spot
the lieutenant decided that it was suitable for the presidio; but he
delayed moving the people there, as he was waiting day by day for
the arrival of the packet."

It is clear from Palóu's account that Lieutenant Moraga selected
the site for the presidio, and that it was not the same site which
Anza had chosen for the fort. Moraga, in his general statement,
says: "The place where the fort is situated, although it is not the
most level in its entire extent, yet it is one of those most protected
from the strong wind which prevails here and one of those nearest
to the [harbor]. No arroyo runs close to it, but with a well which I

---

article entitled, "The Founding of the Presidio and Mission of Our Father Saint
Francis." [Being Chapter 45 of Fray Francisco Palóu's Life of the Venerable Padre
Fray Junípero Serra, Written at the Mission of San Francisco de Asis, and Newly
Translated from the Original Edition of 1787 by George Ezra Dane]. This is an excellent translation except for the regrettable error that Mr. Dane has made in rendering "15 Tiendas de Campaña" as "15 bell-shaped tents", evidently because he con-
fused the word *campaña* as an individual word with the use of it in the expression
"tienda de campaña". Also Dane somehow omitted the two citizen settlers or colonists,
mentioned as "dos Vecinos Pobladores" in the original, who were left with the six
soldiers at the mission (see below, note 140; also see Appendix, p. 136, Ayala's Map
of the Bay, *Explicacion*, item H, for the location of the *Ensenada de los Llorones*).

had opened on a slope very close to the presidio, I discovered a spring sufficient for all necessities and which would be superabundant even though there were a larger number of families. Firewood is abundant and close by, and not far away there is a lake suitable for washing the clothing."[139]

Father Palóu continues: "Seeing that [the ship] did not appear for a whole month, and as they wrote from Monterey, by the pack train which went to bring provisions, that it had sailed long ago, the lieutenant decided to move to that spot so that the soldiers might begin to build their huts for shelter, since it was nearer at hand for making a beginning of the houses. This he did on the 26th of July, setting to work immediately to construct some tule huts. The first was the one that was to serve as chapel, and in it I said Mass on the 28th of the same month.

"Notwithstanding that the order of the commander, which was sent from San Diego to the lieutenant, was to found the presidio only, yet, seeing that he had plenty of men, among soldiers and settlers; that the site of the first mission was so near the presidio; and that as far as he had observed the heathen in the vicinity there was no reason at that time to fear them, as they had shown signs of friendship, the lieutenant decided that we two missionaries should remain, with a guard of six soldiers, all the cattle, and the other things belonging to the mission, so that hand might be put to cutting timbers for a dwelling; and he charged the soldiers and one settler to do the same, so as to have a place to live in with their families."[140]

Meanwhile, the good ship *San Carlos* was having a most remarkable voyage. She was forced by contrary winds and currents to the parallel of San Diego, "but far from the coast." From there she worked north to latitude 42°, then approached the coast and on the

---

[139] See Bolton, *Anza*, III, for "Moraga's Account of the Founding of San Francisco" —Letter of Lieutenant Don Josef Joachín Moraga in Which He Reports the Occupation of the Port of San Francisco, the Erection of a Mission, the Country Explored and Other Achievements. Pp. 409–420. For this translation, Professor Bolton used a certified copy dated Mexico, March 20, 1777, signed by the copyist Melchor de Peramás. In this account Moraga mentions a "plan" which showed the layout of the presidio, but the plan did not, as stated, accompany the Ms and is presumed lost.

[140] Here the Palóu accounts vary: in the *Historical Memoirs*, one settler is mentioned; in the *Life of Serra*, two.

17th of August, almost a month after having departed from Monterey, dropped anchor between Pt. Reyes and the northern farallones. On the 18th of August, at about two o'clock in the afternoon she entered the harbor and "anchored not very far from the spot where the soldiers were lodged, but not in sight of them, as the view was cut off by the point of the hill on whose skirts the camp was placed; but it was in sight of the white cliff and the entrance to the harbor.

"As soon as the bark was made fast, the commander, pilots, and Father Nocedal went ashore.When they saw the site of the camp they were all of the opinion that it was a very suitable place for the fort and presidio, and they thought the same of the site of the Laguna de los Dolores for the mission. In view of the opinion of the captain of the bark and the pilots, work was begun on the building of the houses and the presidio. A square measuring ninety-two varas each way was marked out for it, with divisions for church, royal offices, warehouses, guardhouse, and houses for soldier settlers, a map of the plan being formed and drawn by the first pilot.

"And so that the work might be done as speedily as possible, the commander designated a squad of sailors and the two carpenters to join the servants of the royal presidio in making a good warehouse in which to keep the provisions, a house for the commanding officer of the presidio, and a chapel for celebrating the holy sacrifice of the Mass, while the soldiers were making their own houses for their families.

"The work on the presidio being now under way, Captain Don Fernando Quirós came to the site of the mission, accompanied by the chaplain, a pilot, the surgeon, and six sailors, to aid in building a church or chapel in which to celebrate Mass and a room to live in. With this assistance the buildings were begun, and everything progressed so well that by the middle of September the soldiers had their houses already made of logs, all with flat roofs; the lieutenant had his government house; and a warehouse was finished of the same material, large enough to store all the provisions brought by the bark.

"It was then decided that the formal act of possession should take place, the day appointed for it being that on which our Mother Church celebrates the impression of the stigmata of Our Seraphic Father San Francisco, that is, the 17th of September, a most appropriate day, since he is the patron of the harbor, the new presidio, and the mission. And for taking formal possession of the mission the 4th of October was designated, which is the day dedicated to Our Seraphic Father San Francisco. The commander of the packet, his two pilots, and the greater part of the crew were present at the ceremony of taking formal possession [*of the presidio site*], only those who were absolutely necessary remaining on board; and with the people from the presidio, troops as well as citizens, they made up a goodly number of Spaniards. They were also present four friar priests, all of our College, that is, the two missionary ministers of this mission, the chaplain of the bark, and Father Fray Tomás de la Peña, who had come from Monterey to examine the site for the second mission, of which he had been named minister.

"A solemn Mass was sung by the ministers, and when it was concluded the gentlemen performed the ceremony of taking formal possession. This finished, all entered the chapel and sang the *Te Deum Laudamus*, accompanied by peals of bells and repeated salvos of cannon, muskets, and guns, the bark responding with its swivel-guns, whose roar and the sound of the bells doubtless terrified the heathen, for they did not allow themselves to be seen for many days. The ceremony concluded, the commander of the presidio invited to it all the people, conducting himself with all the splendor that the place permitted, and supplying with his true kindness what would have been missed in other parts, for which all the people were grateful, expressing their gratitude in the joy and happiness which all felt on that day."

The "joy and happiness" which all presumably shared must have been modified to some extent in the case of Lieutenant Moraga who had violated his clear instructions from Commandant Rivera by beginning the construction of the San Francisco mission. Also by the time he got around to writing a letter of explanation for his actions to the Viceroy, Moraga had undertaken still another exploration of the "Rio de San Francisco." So his letter to the Viceroy became an apologia, though as it turned out, everyone was delighted with what Moraga and the soldier-settlers had accomplished. "All this, Most Excellent Sir", wrote Moraga, "I have done without orders from Captain Don Fernando Ribera, but two reasons have been sufficient to oblige me to proceed in this manner. In the first place, I knew the Catholic fervor with which your Excellency looks upon these establishments and that to await in them an order which would delay me would be to run the risk that the just indignation of your Excellency might attribute to lack of due haste what was only obedience.

"In the second place, Don Fernando de Ribera was at the presidio of San Diego, and I had too few men to send a courier so far. And even assuming that it should be decided to send one, while he was going and returning I would lose the best opportunity, which was the aid of the bark, and I would run the risk that, the rains beginning, it would not be possible to erect any building until the following year, which would be most disappointing to the reverend fathers who spiritually succor us here. I protest, Most Excellent Sir, that this my decision had no other purpose than to fulfill as soon as possible the wishes of your Excellency, and that such miserable heathen may have the advantage which so Catholic a breast seeks for them, that is, that without delay they may receive this spiritual good which your Excellency desires for them. If I have done wrong, I humbly beg the charity of your Excellency to mitigate my guilt with the sincerity of my intention. I beg this for the love of God, to whose divine Majesty I pray that in greatest prosperity He may spare the life of your Excellency the many years which these your humble soldiers need for their support."[141]

Lieutenant Moraga had carried through with the program of building the new establishments according to both the letter and the spirit of the Viceregal design. It is perhaps idle to speculate why Lieutenant-Colonel Anza could not have been the one to write the above apology.

Moraga had taken equal delight in the progress being made at both the presidio and mission sites, and it was decided to hold the formal ceremony of the founding of the mission the 4th of October.

---

[141] Bolton, *Anza*, III, "Moraga's Account".

The mission church had been completed and was described by Father Palóu as being eighteen varas long, built of wood, covered with clay, and with a roof of tule (as was the house of the missionaries) "with a room for the sacristy behind the altar, and adorned as well as possible with cloths and drapery and with the banners and pennants of the bark". The chapel was blessed with all ceremony on the 3rd of October, "the Eve of Our Seraphic Father," recorded Palóu, "it being our intention to celebrate the occasion on the following day with all solemnity. But, as the lieutenant had not returned from his expedition at the end of the day, it was agreed to postpone the founding and merely to sing a Mass on the day of Our Seraphic Father, as was done.

"On the 8th of the same month,[142] the lieutenant having arrived the previous afternoon, the ceremony was performed, in the presence of the gentlemen of the bark and all the crew except those required to take care of the vessel, and of the commander of the presidio with all the troops and citizens, only those that were absolutely required remaining in the fort. I sang the Mass with the ministers, and at its conclusion a procession was formed, in which an image of Our Seraphic Father San Francisco, patron of the port, presidio, and mission, was carried on a frame. The function was celebrated with repeated salvos of muskets, rifles, and the swivel-guns that were brought from the bark for this purpose, and also with rockets. All the people who were present at the ceremony remained at the mission to dine, two beeves having been killed for their entertainment. In the afternoon the men re-

---

[142] It is almost certain that the correct formal founding date for Mission San Francisco de Asís is 9 October and not 8 October as is stated in the Palóu *Historical Memoirs*. Geiger, *The Life and Times of Junípero Serra*, II, pp. 140–141, reminds us that the original of the Palóu *Historical Memoirs* is missing, that the copy made by Francisco García Figueroa of Palóu's work in 1792 was accomplished with difficulty because of Palóu's handwriting, about which Figueroa complained. Father Geiger then points out that in other works, notably the *Relación histórica* . . . (Life of Father Serra), the date 9 October is used. Especially in Palóu's document, "Report on the Mission of Our Father, St. Francis, at the Port of the same name from the time of its Founding until the year 1781 included," it is stated, "This mission of Our Holy Father, St. Francis . . . was not established . . . until October 9, 1776. . . . This expedition arrived successfully at the Port of Our Holy Father St. Francis and founded the presidio or fort on September 17 of the said year of 1776; and on October 9 of the said year founded this mission."

turned to the presidio and the crew went on board, the day having been a very joyous one for all. The heathen were the only ones who did not enjoy this happy day, as I shall relate at length in the next chapter," wrote Father Palóu.[143]

"The founding of the presidio and the mission concluded, the sea commander decided to prepare the bark for its return to San Blas, ordering wood and water taken on and the necessary ballast loaded. Everything being finished, and the weather favorable, it safely left this harbor on the morning of the 21st of October. The mission had been successfully founded, not only through the presence of the gentlemen at the function, but also with the aid of some sailors, who assisted in the building, and of the carpenter, who made the doors of the church and house, and a table with two drawers for the altar. Besides this, a gift was made of a *cayuco* and a net for fishing. At the same time it was arranged that four sailors should remain as laborers, completing the number of six who were allowed by his Excellency. With this reënforcement the work proceeded on the buildings and in preparing the land for planting. Crops were put in, and a good stream of water for irrigating was conducted by a ditch which passes close to the houses."[144]

A principal supporter of a mission for San Francisco, Father Junípero Serra, was not able to participate in the actual founding ceremonies because of troubles at San Diego which had demanded his presence there. Serra, as noted, had finally accepted the "new" Bay as the "true" Bay of St. Francis. But in October, 1776, still in San Diego, Serra was not yet aware that the presidio and mission at San Francisco had been founded.[145]

At the very time that Lieutenant Moraga was carrying through with the project of founding the Royal Presidio of San Francisco and Mission San Francisco de Asís, Viceroy Bucareli wrote a long letter to Don Joseph de Gálvez, whose initiative had started the

---

[143] During the first days of San Francisco Mission the natives in the immediate region of the mission all took flight, and it was not until June 24, 1777 that three adult Indians were baptized, "but the rest of the heathen came no more." Palóu, *Historical Memoirs*, Vol. 4, pp. 135–138.

[144] Bolton, *Anza*, III, Palóu's account.

[145] Tibesar, *op. cit.*, III, #107, Serra to Bucareli, 8 October 1776.

entire program for the colonization of Upper California. His August 27, 1776, letter pointed out that Lieutenant-colonel Don Juan Bautista de Anza had now returned to the presidio of Horcasitas in Sonora, "having completed the duties of his commission." Later in this same letter the Viceroy complained that the commission of Anza was "directed principally to the establishment of the presidio projected for the port of San Francisco, with two missions in the neighborhood designed to attract the heathen Indians who live there, but the results have not corresponded to what I hoped for from such careful preparation."

He then commented on the San Diego trouble which had caused Anza to suspend his journey to San Francisco so as to assist Commander Rivera; and that Rivera had conferred his authority to Lieutenant Moraga; that Moraga and Anza had made their explorations and the latter had made his recommendations as to sites; and that "I would have had double the pleasure if [these reports] had been accompanied by the principal item, namely that a beginning had been made of the settlement of the land with the families taken from Sonora, and of the construction of the fort mentioned, as a sign that those lands belong to his Majesty. In this matter the proceedings were not what they ought to have been, as I have indicated with displeasure to Lieutenant-colonel Don Juan Bautista de Ansa and to the commander of those possession, Don Fernando de Rivera y Moncada."

The letter concluded in a more hopeful vein, because the Viceroy heartily endorsed the King's decision that "the governor of the Peninsula should go to reside in Monterrey."

"I immediately communicated to Lieutenant-colonel Don Felipe Neve the royal order concerning the matter, strictly requiring of him its most prompt fulfillment. And subsequently, in view of what was done by Ansa, I have repeated my orders to Neve, manifesting to him how urgent is his removal to that post, both to make the service more pleasing to his Majesty, and for the maintenance and promotion of those new acquisitions. I have told him that at once upon his arrival he must put before everything else the establishment of the presidio and missions at San Francisco, proposing to me in the future whatever he may think best, in agreement with the father president of the missions, Fray Junípero Serra, who knows those regions and always wishes what is best, because of the fervor and apostolic zeal which animates him.

"I thought it wise to send to that governor in brief résumé a report of the difficulties between Don Fernando Rivera and Don Juan Bautista de Ansa, which have contributed much to the failure of my measures, telling him how displeased I am by the dissensions which arose, and that I was appeased solely by the consideration that his presence would afford a remedy for everything, making my measures effective by their fulfillment, and I trust in the zeal and love which this officer has always manifested for the service that everything will be done exactly, without any other such misfortunes as the setback that has been suffered in a matter of such importance."[146]

Even though Commander Rivera could not have learned about the Viceroy's letter to Gálvez, one can imagine his trepidation when he received in September, 1776, still at San Diego, a letter from the Viceroy which presupposed that the two missions of the Port of San Francisco had been founded. "The fact was that the commandant not only had not even begun to establish them, but also had with him the twelve soldiers assigned to them. Thus he was in quite an anxious state of mind, and in order to resolve his difficulty, he took to the road with those soldiers to found the missions. When he arrived in Monterey, he learned that this Mission of San Francisco, Our Father, had already been founded. In order to found the second, together with Father Fray Tomás de la Peña, one of the missionaries assigned to it, he came to survey the territory." Thus wrote Father Palóu in his *Life of Serra*.[147]

Commander Rivera and Father Peña then picked the site for future Mission Santa Clara, and afterwards proceeded to San Francisco where they arrived on the 26th of November. Rivera then inspected the mission and the presidio and ratified everything that Lieutenant Moraga had done. Rivera and Moraga made a brief

---

[146] Bolton, *Anza*, V, Document #XCIII.

[147] Geiger, *op. cit.*, Ch. XLVI, p. 196. Palóu, *Noticias*, IV, p. 154, states that Commander Rivera learned about the founding of Mission San Francisco before he reached Monterey; namely, at Mission San Luis Obispo.

exploration of the *contra costa*; Rivera then proceeded to Monterey and from there sent soldiers and their families to the presidio of San Francisco where they arrived near the end of December. Now Lieutenant Moraga was again cast in the role of founder, and with Father Peña and the colonists traveled from San Francisco to Santa Clara where, 12 January 1777, Father Tomás de la Peña sang the first Mass at Mission Santa Clara de Asís.[148] In a manner of speaking, San Francisco was already having an offshoot colony!

Later that year the Father President, Junípero Serra, visited Santa Clara where he preached and celebrated High Mass on September 29; then at daybreak, October 1st he set out for San Francisco, walking all that day and part of the night to reach Mission San Francisco de Asís. There, on the feast of San Francisco, October 4, Serra celebrated High Mass and preached. He remained in the Mission for ten days, and during his stay visited the presidio. When there, he exclaimed: "Thanks be to God. Now Our Father St. Francis, the crossbearer in the procession of missions, has come to the final point of the mainland of California; for in order to go farther, ships will be necessary."[149]

Thus, from the first sighting of the Bay by Sergeant Ortega and his exploring party, 1 November 1769, until the founding of the San Francisco Presidio and Mission, in September and October 1776, and the "ratification" of their foundings by Commandant Rivera in November 1776, barely seven years had elapsed.

In this brief time an immense amount of space had been traversed by land and by sea in the explorations preliminary to the San Francisco foundations; and an even greater distance had been traveled by despatches and royal orders, back and forth across the Atlantic. The amount of paperwork involved was simply colossal!

The end result, however, was that for Spain certain symbols had been planted at the end of the peninsula which Serra had called the "final point of the California mainland." These symbols were not alone the Cross and the Sword. They were also the Mattock, and

---

[148] Geiger, *ibid.*, p. 142.

[149] John A. Berger, *The Franciscan Missions of California* (1941), pp. 312–313, for mention of Serra's pedestrian abilities and fortitude. The Serra quotation is found in Geiger, *ibid.*, p. 209.

the Plow, and the Branding-iron, for the Spanish program was one of true colonization in which their own countrymen were directly involved and in which the local residents, the "heathen" Indians, were expected to share.[150]

The distances from the settled areas in New Spain were so great that a massive population movement to the San Francisco peninsula never occurred. Probably it was never intended that it should. The program initiated by Gálvez was in its inception one of forestalling the actions of others, mainly the Russians, who soon enough did reach the Bay region but who could not, because of Spain's prior accomplishment, settle themselves on the very shores of the Bay itself.

The prophecy of Father Font, expressed in his diary on 28 March 1776, that the end of the peninsula had the best advantages "for founding in it a most beautiful city" was never realized for Spain. The beginnings were there, however, in the presidio, the missions, the people, the seeds, plants, and livestock.

Also there was the name, San Francisco, which Visitor Gálvez had seen in the Cabrera Bueno *derrota*, and which was given to this Spanish *march* on the occasion when the Royal Presidio of San Francisco was officially founded, 17 September 1776.

---

[150] There is a huge literature on the "Indian" and "mission" questions. It may be remarked that, no matter what the method employed, any form of European invasion of Indian country brought ultimate ruination to the Indian. The Spanish concept of the "good Indian" was a docile, Christianized Indian with whom he intermarried. The Spanish sense of a civilizing mission was staunchly believed in by the missionaries, in the case of Alta California, the Franciscans from the San Fernando College. The "good Indian—dead Indian" formula of the Anglo-Americans of later years was starkly at variance with the Spanish attitude toward the "heathen." See especially the writings of S. F. Cook, for example, "The Conflict Between the California Indians and White Civilization" in *Ibero-Americana*: 21–24 (1943).

Appendixes

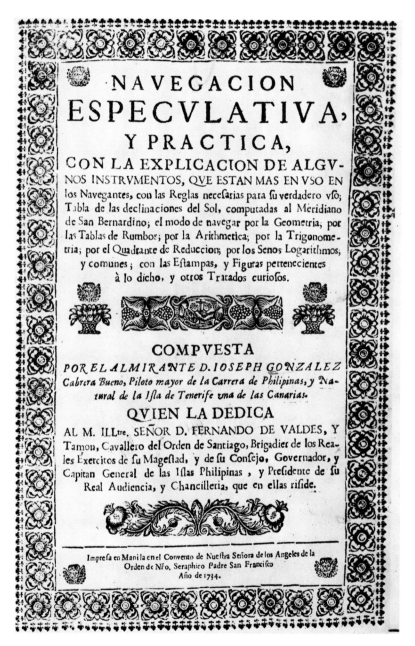

NAVEGACION ESPECVLATIVA, Y PRACTICA,

CON LA EXPLICACION DE ALGV-

NOS INSTRVMENTOS, QVE ESTAN MAS EN VSO EN los Navegantes, con las Reglas necesarias para su verdadero vso; Tabla de las declinaciones del Sol, computadas al Meridiano de San Bernardino; el modo de navegar por la Geometria; por las Tablas de Rumbos; por la Arithmetica; por la Trigonome-tria; por el Quadrante de Reduccion; por los Senos Logarithmos, y comunes; con las Estampas, y Figuras pertenecientes à lo dicho, y otros Tratados curiosos.

COMPVESTA

POR EL ALMIRANTE D. IOSEPH GONZALEZ Cabrera Bueno, Piloto mayor de la Carrera de Philipinas, y Na-tural de la Isla de Tenerife una de las Canarias.

QVIEN LA DEDICA

AL M. ILLtre. SEÑOR D. FERNANDO DE VALDES, Y Tamon, Cavallero del Orden de Santiago, Brigadier de los Rea-les Exercitos de su Magestad, y de su Consejo, Governador, y Capitan General de las Islas Philipinas , y Presidente de su Real Audiencia, y Chancilleria, que en ellas riside.

Impresa en Manila en el Convento de Nuestra Señora de los Angeles de la Orden de Nro. Seraphico Padre San Francisco Año de 1734.

APPENDIX I

Title Page of the *Navegacion Especulativa, y Practica*

✥) CAPIT. IV. (✥

Derrota deſde el Cabo de Mendocino, haſta el Puerto de Acapulco por la Coſta.

EN Altura de 41. grados, eſtà vn Cabo de tierra grueſſa al parecer taxado à la mar, y del ſe corre la Coſta de tierra mas mediana coſa de ocho leguas, la buelta del Sur donde haze la tierra, otra Punta de tierra grueſſa, pelada con algunas Barrancas blancas que caen ſobre la mar, y eſtà eſta Punta, en 41. grados y medio, y llamaſe el Cabo Mendocino, de aqui corre la Coſta al Sueſte haſta altura de 39. grados y medio, tierra de mediana altura muy poblada de Arboleda, con algunas Lomas pequeñas, peladas por la orilla dela mar. En eſtà altura ſuſodicha, haze vna Punta baxa, de Barrancas blancas, taxadas a la mar; y de aqui corre la Coſta al Sueſte quarta al Sur haſta llegar à 38. grados y medio donde haze la tierra, vna Punta mediana dividida de la Coſta, que parece deſde lejos Isla, y ſella ma Punta de los Reyès, laqual haze vn Morro taxado, y de la parte del Norte de ella, haze buen abrigo para todos vientos, y eſta en altura de 38. grados y medio, que llaman de S. Franciſco, para viento Sur, y Sueſte, ſe à de Surgir en el remate de la Playa ǫ haze vn rincon de la parte del Sudueſte, y de la parte del Nordeſte, eſtàn tres Bar-

ran-

The section of the Cabrera Bueno *Derrota* wherein is found reference to the "buen abrigo" from all winds, called S. Francisco, formed by the steep *Morro* known as the *Punta de los Reyès*.

THE CABRERA BUENO "DERROTA"
(CAPE MENDOCINO TO ACAPULCO)

Translated excerpt from the "Derrota desde el Cabo de Mendocino, hasta el Puerto de Acapulco por la Costa" from Capitulo IV
in the Quinta Parte de la Navegacion in Joseph Gonzalez Cabrera
Bueno, *Navegacion Especulativa, y Practica* . . . (Manila, 1734):*

"In latitude 42° is a high cape, seemingly cut off at the sea, and from it
runs a lower coast some eight leagues southward, where the land forms
another high point, bare, with some white cliffs which fall off to the sea;
this point is in 41°30′, and is called Cape Mendocino. From here the
coast runs to the southeast, one quarter south as far as 38°30′, where the
land forms a point of medium height separated from the coast, which
appears from a distance to be an island, and is called *Punta de los Reyes*.
It forms a steep cliff, and on its north side[*i.e.*, north side of the eastern
promontory of Pt. Reyes headland] affords a good shelter from all winds.
This harbor [*abrigo*] is in latitude 38°30′ and is called San Francisco. In a
south or southeast wind the anchorage is at the end of the shore where it
forms an angle on the southwest; and on the northeast there are three
white cliffs [*barrancas blancas*] very close to the sea and opposite the
middle one an *estero* enters from the sea which has a good entrance without any breakers. Upon entering, there will be found friendly Indians,
and fresh water may easily be obtained. To the south-southwest of this
port are six or seven small white farallones, some larger than others, occupying in circuit a little more than a league. Anyone who comes from
Cape Mendocino on the look-out for this port when six leagues at sea
from the Cape will turn southeast, one quarter south, will arrive at Pt.
Reyes and will see the farallones, which is a good landmark for recogniz-
ing it. Here is where was lost the *Navio S. Agustin* in 1595, coming to
make the discovery, and the cause of shipwreck was more because of him
who steered than the force of the weather. . . . "

---

* See reproduction of title page, p. 103.

las expediciones que se intentan hacer en
614.546.873.377.842.135.352.384.380.943.767.874.169.874.143.788.
continuacion de los Descubrimientos en aquellas
882.664.908.996.643.790.764.135.380.1025.560.874.157.158.814.998.
partes viendo que será el modo de abrir
361.134.546.1031.934.874.335.340.576.124.363.680.300.169.874.340.
este Imperio un nuevo ramo de comercio que
995.238.300.562.546.115.339.874.574.786.316.355.760.994.707.340.
se lisonjean les sera muy útil, no obstante
238.297.881.321.339.380.43.1031.874.930.175.310.284.1017.874.340.
la grande distancia que hay por tierra por
132.354.790.718.768.844.94.882.786.854.399.994.735.882.390.20.
la brevedad del Veren que es el mar que
169.135.361.334.339.879.108.850.114.620.387.298.797.996.1031.997.
puede estar dehelado en aquellos parages –
588.116.994.564.997.960.167.663.854.300.996.632.1031.334.874.335.
y la incertidumbre del espacio que hay
340.577.150.850.143.908.790.385.236.144.298.997.335.380.943.166.
hasta la California, que es el Pais recono-
546.144.718.84.792.850.374.195.930.748.339.680.74.56.1031.997.
cido que hay por aquella parte.
995.335.361.874.381.768.380.300.1031.750.334.339.632.166.932.

115.994.1055.107.

Hro. S. Que a V. E. m. a. Moscou 34/20 de Nov.re de 1767.

Exmo. Sr.
B. L. M. de V. E.
su mas atento reconocido
Servidor.
Vizconde de la Herreria

Exmo. Sr. Marques de Grimaldi.

APPENDIX 3

Coded message (last page), Herriára to Grimaldi, 1767 (Russia in the
North Pacific)

PLAN FOR THE ERECTION OF A GOVERNMENT AND GENERAL COMMANDANCY

(Prepared by Visitor Joseph de Gálvez and Viceroy Marqués de Croix. Adapted from I. B. Richman, *op. cit.*, and checked against the Microfilm, Bancroft Library, in *AGN*, Provincias Internas, 154)

If, since the glorious Conquest which the great Hernan Cortés made of the broad Domains which come under the name of Nueva España, effort had been made by his Successors in this Government to Second and to carry out the Lofty designs of that Hero, the Light of the Gospel and the supremacy of the August Kings of España would have reached even to the utmost Bounds, not yet known, of this immense Continent. But as the spirit of activity and of Conquest was extinguished with the life of that inimitable Man, with his death came to an end the rapid advances which he accomplished in this new World; and at last we have not even maintained and conserved the possession which we enjoyed, in undisturbed tranquillity, of the richest territories on the Frontiers of Sonora and Nueva Vizcaya.

The more immediate (and perhaps the exact) causes of this failure, and of the veritable ruin which has befallen the unfortunate inhabitants of those Provinces, with grave injury to the State, are, in reality, the utter neglect with which they have been regarded at Mexico in these latter years; the considerable distance at which they are situated, more than Six Hundred Leagues, from this Capital; and the pressing Crowd of more immediate business and cares which engross the entire attention of any Viceroy of Nueva España. For, as he is not supplied with Subordinates to assist him, it is not possible for him to make active provision, or for the influence of his authority to be felt, at the remote confines of an almost boundless Empire.

This practical knowledge which the present Viceroy has been acquiring, with no less discomfort than hardship, and the favorable opportunity afforded to him by the present expedition to Sonora, have made him reflect very seriously on the means which may be most suitable and efficacious for reestablishing this great Monarchy in its earlier prosperity, and to put the distant Provinces into condition for maintaining themselves with Vigor, and for enlarging the [Spanish] domination—extending at the same time the Catholic Faith, in acknowledgment and reward for which God is allotting to the Crown of Espana the Richest Empires of the Universe.

With this view, then, of establishing in the uncultivated Provinces of this [new] world good order and Justice, and the opulence which is natural for them if they are placed under proper management, he proposes, and sends to the Viceroy by this post, another and separate Plan for Intendancies, in imitation of those which exist in the Metropolitan Province. And to the end that Our Sovereign the King may secure the important advantages of quickly aggrandizing the Rich Frontiers of this Empire, he has come to an agreement with the Vistador-General to develop the idea of a General Commandancy, suitably empowered, which shall comprehend under its exclusive administration the aforesaid Provinces of Sonora, Sinaloa, Nueva Vizcaya, and the Peninsula of Californias. That region will now begin to recognize the Spanish Power, and to repay part of the great amount that it has cost the Crown and the Nation since its discovery and the foundation of the first Jesuit Missions.

What has most contributed to this idea—which the Viceroy and the Vistador regard as very serviceable, and its execution as quite indispensable—is the previously planned decision which has been reached in Council, and fully approved, that the Vistador shall go to establish Settlements in the said Provinces, and organize the Government of the latter with full powers and Commission from the Viceroy. The object of this action is to facilitate and hasten the erection of such Government and Commandancy upon the footing which is proposed in this Plan, since obstacles can never arise between two faithful Servants of the King who, Moving toward the same end, with upright intentions, always agree in their discussions and unite their efforts, with mutual concessions.

In view of these facts, and with the further incentive of having seen a project which was laid before the Lords Ministers of Madrid in December, 1760, for the creation of a Viceroyalty independent from that of Mexico, and including all the Provinces situated in the great district under the jurisdiction of the Audiencia of Guadalaxara, the Viceroy and the Visitador have concluded that it will be much more advantageous and less expensive to establish an authorized Government and General Commandancy in the three frontier Provinces. For [such a Government], possessing all the powers necessary to maintain them free from the invasions of the Barbarians, and gradually to extend their boundaries, will render them of use to their Sovereign Master; and it will be responsible only to the Chief who represents him in these Domains, and subordinate to him only so far as to report Affairs to him and to request his aid when that may be necessary.

In this manner will be avoided the difficulties, always odious, which usually arise over jurisdiction or limits between coordinate officials when they have similar duties; and by surrendering to the Commandancy of the Frontier Provinces the entire authority—which is indispensable in regions so far distant, in order not to cause failure in opportunities and in the most important projects—the exceedingly important object will be attained of furnishing life and movement to regions so extensive, fruitful and rich by Nature, which can in a few years form a New Empire, equal or even superior to this one of Mexico.

Nor are these advantages and utilities, although great, the only ones which the proposed new Government will yield; for as soon as the activity of a Commandant with authority and energy is felt, many dangers can be averted which now threaten us, by way of the South Sea, from certain foreign Powers who now have an opportunity and the most eager desire to establish some Colony at the Port of Monterrey, or at some other of the many harbors which have already been discovered on the western Coasts of this new World.

In this report is purposely omitted extended discussion of the continual attempts by which France and England have striven, for some two centuries, to find a passage from the Northern to the Southern Sea—especially by their Colonies in this North America—and of the exertions that the Russians are making, through the Sea of Tartary, to penetrate into our Indias. This is partly because Field-Marshal Don Antonio Ricardos departed from here the year before, with the purpose of presenting an elaborate Memorial on these facts, which are more easy to verify in Europe; and partly because the Prime Minister of España knows very well that the English—who now, as a result of the last War, are Masters of Canada and a great part of Luciana [Louisiana]—will spare no expense, diligence, or hardship to push forward the discoveries which the French made through those Colonies, a new Viceroyalty. It has seemed proper to put forth this idea clearly, for the reasons above explained, as well as to avoid so great expenses, when the same results can be obtained by means of the Commandancy which is proposed in this Plan.

Nor is it reckoned expedient that the new Governor and Commander-in-Chief establish his residence in the City of Durango, the Capital of Nueva Vizcaya, as was proposed in the year 1760—not only because that Town is very distant from Sonora, and much farther from the Californias, which at the present time need an active and continual promotion; but because (from the necessity of stationing an Intendant in Durango, if the Separate Plan which is sent be approved), the establishment which is therein proposed would be in any event less advantageous [at Durango].

For the Governors who have hitherto administered Nueva Viscaya have all (excepting the present one) lived in the Town of San Felipe de Chihuahua, which is the Frontier settlement and a very important Mining Centre, where the presence of a Governor who can defend it is certainly needed.

In this connection, likewise, [it may be noted] that for the present the Audiencia of Guadalaxara remains in that Capital, expenses which would assuredly be caused by its transfer; and if in the course of time (which must make known the benefits that the General Commandancy will produce) it shall seem expedient, as it may, to locate the Superior Tribunal of Nueva Galicia, or to erect another, in the Capital which is to be established in Sonora, it would be very easy to carry out that plan then at little expense, and with the knowledge which experience furnishes in all human affairs.

What is judged to be certainly indispensable, and to be immediately effected, is the erection of a central Settlement on the confines of Sonora—either on the shore of the Gila River, or very near it (arrangements being meanwhile made to set up the Government at the Mission of Caborca, as being the station most advanced toward the Frontier), or else at the junction of that River and the Colorado. Then, the Capital of the New Government being located at almost equal distances from the Californias and Nueva Vizcaya, its Chief with his administrative measures can proceed to either Province with the same ease—and indeed he ought to travel through them and visit all places, in order that by examining them with his own eyes, and gaining specific knowledge from being actually in the field, he may be enabled to shape his course with good judgment.

No less necessary and useful will be a Mint, which ought to be erected in that same Capital of Sonora, in order that Commerce may have free course, to the benefit of the public and of the Royal Treasury; and that the poor Vassals who have settled in those remote regions may not be under the painful necessity of transporting all the Gold and Silver to Mexico. [This they have done], with only damages and great expenses which utterly ruin them, or, when not so heavy, deprive them of the profits which the richness of the Ores would allow them if they could sell those metals in the same Region where they dig and Smelt them. And, lest it be feared that the establishment of a Mint in that Province would cause notable diminution in the output of the Mint at Mexico, that of Sonora could be restricted to the coining of only a Million *pesos* each year; for that sum would be sufficient at present to supply that province with Money and to give a like share to the Californias and Nueva Vizcaya—

where, in truth, through the lack of Money, the King is suffering a great diminution in his Imposts, and the inhabitants intolerable grievances.

In the Capital which should be founded, a Bishop's See also ought to be erected, setting aside for the support of this New Dignity the Province of Sonora, also Sinaloa (which belongs to the Bishopric of Durango, and is at the considerable distance of more than Two Hundred and Fifty leagues), and the Peninsula of Californias. Although the last-named, as is claimed, is included in the Diocese of Guadalaxara, neither the reverend Bishops nor their Vistadors ever possessed any acquaintance with it; and consequently neither is the See of Nueva Galicia injured by the separation of Californias, nor is the loss which that of Durango will actually experience by cutting off from it Sonora and Sinaloa worthy of consideration, for in those territories there are very few Curates and the tithes are almost nothing. But these will very soon be increased, with the Government and General Commandancy in the undeveloped territories which are assigned to the new Bishopric.

It would be idle to enumerate the great [advantages] which the Bishop's See that is proposed in the Metropolis of Sonora would confer on Religion and the state; for the ardent zeal and Apostolic ministry of a Diocesan Prelate would immensely advance the conversion of the Heathen, hastening their reduction by influences near at hand, and conquering many souls for the Creator, at the same pace with which new Domains are acquired for the Sovereign who is His Immediate Vicar in the world. And it is certain that in no part of America are there so fine opportunities and so abundant a harvest as in the confines of Sonora and in the Missions of Californias; for the Tribes of Indians are exceedingly numerous, and their natural disposition renders them most easily persuaded of the infallible truth of the Catholic faith.

In view of these just considerations, the erection of the new See should not be considered a burden, even though it might be necessary at the beginning to assist the Prelate and his limited Church with some revenue from the Royal Treasury; for such pension would not continue long, when we consider the natural fertility of those lands—which, placed under cultivation, will yield the most abundant produce—and just as certainly would the Royal Estate be repaid [for this outlay] and even much more, on account of the richness of the Mines in those Provinces, which are well understood and known by all.

As to what is proper for the General Commandant, it is proposed that he should be independent of the Audiencia and President of Guadalaxara; and it would be necessary to confer on him the salary of twenty thousand *pesos*, in order that he may have barely means on which to live with any [suitable] display in those remote regions, and to meet the expenses of his journeys from one Province to another, without its being necessary for him to avail himself of the [extra] imposts, [now] condemned, which have been tolerated in the Indias, and which have brought them into the melancholy decadence which they are suffering up to the present time. If perchance this salary, and those of the three Intendants who in another Plan are proposed by the Californias, Sonora, and Durango, shall seem excessive, it will be easy to make it evident by experience that the Treasury will be well indemnified for the amount of all these expenses. For after the second year from the establishment of these positions the amount allotted to them certainly cannot reach even the tenth part of the increase which will appear in one branch of revenue alone, the fifths of the Silver and the Gold which may be dug and smelted in Sonora and Californias. To this must be added the revenue from the Pearls; from the fishery, although it might be very abundant on the Coasts of that Peninsula, nothing has been thus far produced to the Royal Treasury.

The greatest saving of expense which should be reckoned upon to the benefit of His Majesty is in the very large expense-accounts [*situados*] of the many Garrisons [*Presidios*] which exist in the Californias, Sonora, and Nueva Viscaya; for, as the profitable idea of establishing Settlements on the Frontiers of these Provinces has for its aim to guard them from the invasions of the Infidel Indians, it will result in liberation from the useless and insupportable burden of so many Garrisons, which, as events prove, are of little or no use. For, although six of these are maintained in the Province of Sonora alone, it is more often invaded and more devastated, than the others—because those Garrisons are, in effect, really Rancherias, and chiefly serve to enrich the Captains and their outfitters.

It is true that, in order to garrison the Capital that is projected in Sonora and to guard the chain of Settlements on the Frontiers (which should be quasi-Military), two Companies of Dragoons and three of Mountain Fusileers, each of a hundred men, will be needed; but nothing is easier than to fill out this force by adding fifty recruits to the two [companies?] who have gone on the Sonora expedition. Taking for granted that the expense of these Veteran Bodies hardly reaches the third part of that which is caused at present by the Garrisons, it is clear that the Royal Treasury, thus coming out with much profit, would be able to pay the salaries of the Commandancy and intendancies; and the Frontiers of the three Provinces would be really shielded from the incursions of the Barbarians. For the new Towns, protected by the Squads into which the

Fusileer Companies should be divided, could immediately be put into condition to defend their respective territories, and in time to aid in extending the [Spanish] domination—in view of which, and with these obligations, the Colonists must be established in the new Settlements, giving to each one the Arms necessary for his defense.

With the five Companies of Veteran Infantry and Cavalry, the Militia which the new Towns ought to form, and those who may be recruited in the Town of San Felipe de Chihuahua and its vicinity, it is estimated that the new General Commandant will be able for the present to maintain the defense of the Provinces embraced in his Government. If afterward he shall need, as is probable, larger forces for the expeditions which he will find expedient to send out for the purpose of advancing the Conversions and discoveries, it should not be difficult to increase the troops, either regular or provincial, when experience makes known the great benefits which are promised by this useful establishment in Provinces which are undoubtedly more abundant and rich in mineral products than any others that have been discovered in this Northern America.

Recently news has come that [the English have gone] as far as the Lake of Bois, from which issues the deep-flowing River of the West, directing its course, as discovered, toward the Sea of that name; and if it empties therein, or reaches the South Sea, or is (as may be the case) the famous Colorado River, which forms the Gulf of Californias, there is no doubt, in whichever of these alternatives, that we already have the English very near to our Settlements in New Mexico, and not very distant from the Western Coast of this Continent of America.

Moreover, the Prime Minister of our Court knows, for the voyages and memoirs that are published in Europe, that the Russians have been gaining an intimate knowledge of the navigation of the Sea of Tartary; and that they are, according to very credible and well-grounded statements, carrying on the Fur Trade on a Continent or Island which, it is estimated, lies at the distance of only eight hundred leagues from the Western Coast of Californias, which runs as far as Capes Mendocino and Blanco.

But, while the attempts of Russia and England need not revive at this time all the suspicions and anxieties that Spain manifested in former days (especially after the Reign of Felipe Second) for discovering and gaining possession by way of the South Sea, of the alleged passage which the other Nations were seeking by way of the North Sea, it is undubitable that since the year 1749 [*sic*]—in which Admiral Anson came to the Western Coast of this Kingdom, as far as the entrance to the Port of

Acapulco—the English and the Dutch (who afterward brought their ships from Eastern India within sight of Cape San Lucas and the Coasts of New Galicia) have acquired a very detailed knowledge of the Ports and Bays which we hold on the South Coast, especially in the Peninsula of Californias. With all this no one can regard it as impossible or even very difficult for one of these two Nations or for the Moscovites to establish, when that is least expected, a Colony at the Port of Monterrey, where they would have all desirable facilities and conveniences; and that thus we should come to see our North America invaded and exploited by way of the South Sea as it has been by that of the North.

In these circumstances, it seems as if worldly prudence may counsel, and even carry into effect, that we should take proper precautions in time, putting into practice whatever measures may be feasible to avert the dangers that threaten us. And, as at present the peninsula of Californias is free from obstruction, it follows that we should and easily could—its population being increased by the aid of the free Commerce which ought to be carried on between that territory and this Kingdom—transport a Colony to the Port of Monterrey with the same vessels that we now have in the South Sea, which have been built for the use of the Sonora expedition. It only remains to establish in this Province the General Commandancy, which very soon can promote and facilitate the Settlement of Monterrey, and of other points on the Western Coast of the same Californias—where there are good Harbors, and the soil is more fertile and productive than that of the North Shore.

A chief who is on the ground and energetic will secure considerable extensions to the Frontiers of Sonora and Nueva Viscaya, unless he is insufficiently provided with the funds that are necessary in order that the establishment of his Government may produce the utilities and advantages that ought to be expected. These are set forth at length in the project, already cited, which was presented to the Court in the year 1760, with the aim of securing the erection [of such a Government]. If the decision be reached that it is more expedient to maintain on the Frontiers of Chihuahua an Official, subordinate to the Governor, for the defense of that Mining Centre, a suitable person for that employ is Captain Don Lope de Cuellar, who was appointed by the Viceroy in fulfillment of the instructions addressed to him for the expulsion of the regulars belonging to the Company [of Jesus]. As that measure would do away with the office of *corregidor* that was established in that Town, which enjoys very considerable imposts, from the fund that they produce can be drawn the Salary of two thousand *pesos*, which of course will be an addition to his pay sufficient to maintain the said Governor. At the same time he ought to look after the affairs of the Royal Treasury, with rank as Deputy of the Intendant of Nueva Viscaya—who must reside in the Capital City of Durango, and be, like the Intendants of Sonora and Californias, directly subordinate to the General Commandant of the three Pronvices, since that Chief is responsible for rendering account to the Viceroy of Nueva España of whatever enterprises he may undertake, and of all occurrences worthy of note in the region under his command.

An examination of this plan will make evident at first view that in it are discussed only the principal points and designs of the idea, and that its sole aim, with nothing else in view, is to promote the public Interests of the King and the State in an establishment which, besides the urgent necessity of effecting it, carriers the special recommendation that it will be very advantageous in a short time; for, from now on, the Foundations of the Work are going to be laid with Solidity, Integrity, and Zeal.

At Mexico, the twenty-third of January, [in the year] One Thousand, Seven Hundred, and Sixty-Eight.

DON JOSE DE GALVEZ.

To the Marques de Croix.

THE "CRESPÍ" MAP*

Description on the map

Spanish text

Mapa de lo substancial del Famoso Puerto y Rio de San Francisco explorado por tierra en el Mes de Marzo del presente año de 1772 sacado por el Diario, y Observaciones del R. P. Fr. Juan Crespi Missionero Apostolico del Colegio de propaganda fide de Franciscos Observantes de San Fernando de Mexico, y Ministro de la Nueva Mission de Monterrey. Se omiten los Arroyos corrientes, y dulces, Arboledas, y Rancherias de Gentiles por la precision y ser Mapa abierto. Todo desde la punta del Estero (donde desagua un buen Rio) para adelante abunda much mas; y los Gentiles desde la Bahia arriba se hallaran rubios blancos y barbados y todos muy buenos y afables que regalaron â los Españoles con sus frutas y corridas.

English translation

Map of the main part of the famous Port and River of San Francisco explored by land in the month of March in the present year of 1772, extracted from the diary and observations of the Reverend Father Fray Juan Crespi *Misionero Apostolico del Colegio de propaganda fide de Franciscos Observantes de San Fernando de Mexico, y Ministro de la Nueva Mision de Monterrey.* Omitted are streams of running and sweet water, groves of trees, and Indian settlements, for purposes of necessity and clarity. From the end of the estuary (where debouches a large stream) and beyond there are very many heathen everywhere; and the heathen of the upper bay [*Bahia redonda*] had ruddy complexions and beards and all were very kind and friendly and presented the Spaniards with their fruits and drinks.

---

* Photocopy in Bancroft Library. Chapman *Catalogue* #1842. (*AGI*, Aud. de Guad. p. 512.)

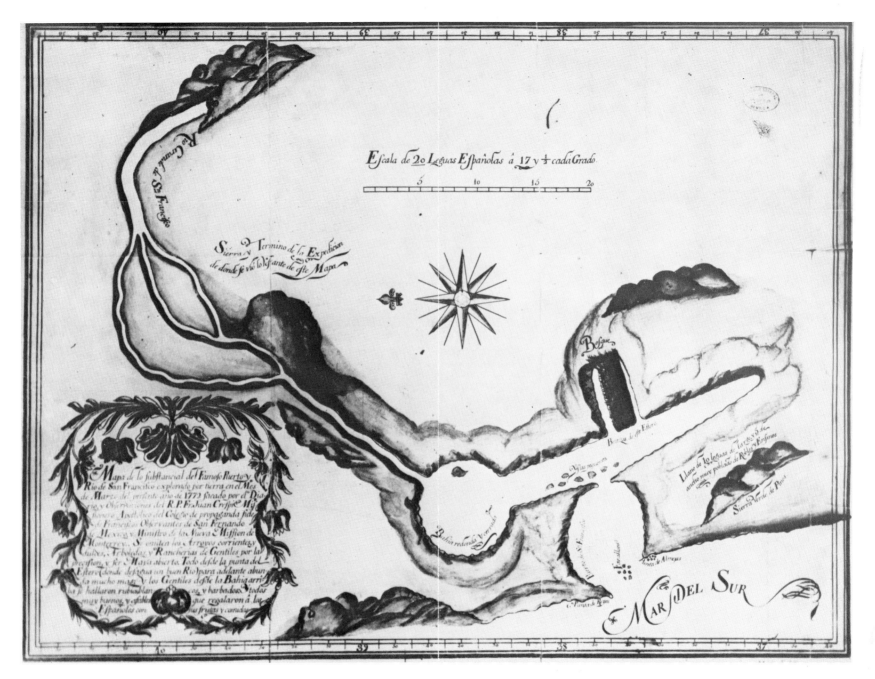

The "Crespi" Map

The Mystery of the "Crespí" Map

A map, known as the "Crespí" Map, has been reproduced in a number of works such as Fray Francisco Palóu, *Historical Memoirs of New California*, Vol. 2, and *Fray Juan Crespí, Missionary Explorer on the Pacific Coast: 1769–1774*, both translated and edited by H. E. Bolton; and in Neal Harlow, *The Maps of San Francisco Bay, from the Spanish Discovery in 1769 to the American Occupation* (The Book Club of California, 1950). Bolton, in *Crespi*, says: "Crespi made a most interesting map of the results of this expedition, the original manuscript of which is in the Archivo General de Indias." He states that the map is reproduced in "this volume" and, thus, accepts the map as of Crespí authorship. Harlow points out in a note that other maps were copied from the original and also quotes from Father Font, of which more later. Harlow also makes the statement in his note that there are references to the map "in the writings."

Henry Raup Wagner, *The Spanish Southwest 1542–1795. An Annotated Bibliography* (Berkeley, 1924) lists Item #13 as "Map of the Port of San Francisco, March 1772, drawn by Fr. Rafael Verger from the observations of Fr. Juan Crespí." No citation or notation accompanies this statement. The same author in *The Cartography of the Northwest Coast of America to the Year 1800* (Berkeley, 1937), Vol. I, p. 171 writes; "Fr. Crespí perhaps made a map of this expedition which we know today in a copy [*sic*] made in Mexico by Fr. Rafael Verger, the guardian of the San Fernando College, although Verger states that he made it from the journal and observations of Fr. Crespí. It is a little crude, being nothing much more than a bird's-eye view of the country from the Contra Costa side of San Francisco Bay . . ." Again, no citation is provided for this commentary.

To untangle the mystery of the map, one is impelled first to go to Crespí's own writings. In this connection it must be noted that Father Crespí was a stickler for detail. Serra himself once wrote to Father Verger, the Franciscan Guardian, that "[Crespí] talks at great length, I admit. On a number of occasions while he was busily engaged with his writing I tried to take the matter in hand—suggesting that he go light on the minutiae, repetitions and superlatives. Putting on a big frown, he would say: 'Then you do not want me to tell things just as they are, or as I saw them?' " (Tibesar, *op. cit.*, I, #20, Monterey, June 20, 1771.)

Hence, it is strange and frustrating indeed to discover that nowhere in his own writings does Father Crespí refer to a map. With respect to this assertion we turn first to the Diaries of the 1772 expedition of which this writer has examined four forms. These are three forms of the Crespí diary, and the "newly-discovered" Fages diary (see above, note #41 for a full discussion of the Fages diary, and references to the Crespí diaries).

In the Palóu-Figueroa version of the Crespí diary, used in the main by Professor Bolton in his *Crespí*, we find a relevant excerpt of the entry for Friday, 27 March, 1772, translated as follows: ". . . We halted a little while in order to map the entry through the gate to the mainland, and it appeared to all of us to run from west to east through the gulf where the seven or more farallones are lined up." The Spanish for this reads: " . . . paramos un rato para demarcar la bocana á la tierra firme, y nos pareció á todos ser del Oeste al Este por dentro de la ensenada en donde están tendidos los siete ó mas farallones." This can be translated: "We halted a short time to demark (or survey) the entrance to the mainland and to all of us it appeared to be from the west to the east on the inside of the ensenada [inlet] where the seven or more farallones are lined up."

It should be noted that in this expedition of 1772 and also in the earlier one of 1769 whenever Father Crespí makes specific reference to "shooting the sun" he does so in words such as, "observé la altura" or "para registrar y vimos", etc. and then provides the degrees and minutes of the latitude. However, in the 31 October 1769 entry he states: "From this beach the farallones lie west by southwest . . ." The Spanish for this is "Desde esta playa se van demarcando los farallones del Oeste cuarta al Sudoeste . . ." Hence, the usage of *demarcar* with reference to the "Gate" in 1772 seems quite similar to his earlier use of that term during the 1769 expedition when no map was being made but during which latitudes and compass bearings were being recorded. This latter is exactly what Crespí describes he is doing during both expeditions. In 1772 the compass bearing of the entrance or mouth of San Francisco Bay is described as west to east. This writer, in the light of Crespi's language usage, finds it impossible to accept "to map the entry through the gate" as a correct translation of the Spanish text quoted.

In the Sevilla Ms, in the Verger-Crespí Ms, and in the Fages diary, the entrance to the Bay is described as running from west to east. In these documents there is no mention at all concerning any "observation" being made.

The only specific mention of a map in the diary literature occurs in the Verger-Crespí version of Crespí's diary (entry for 30 March). At that place in the diary where Crespí explains that the expedition has reached its farthest point, one finds the words: "I shall see if I am able to give [provide] a poor form of this estuary and Rio Grande which will accompany this Diary so that one can understand what it is." However, the Verger-Crespí form of the diary is, in Father Verger's own words, an "explained" form of the Crespí writing; thus, we are not too surprised when at the end of the Diary we find the words—"In agreement with this information I present Your Excellency with a poorly formed map which I made . . ." In other words, Father Verger, who then signs the document, here tells us how he found it useful to prepare a map, even a poor one, so that the Viceroy could the better grasp the meaning of the "estuary" and the great river system which Fages and Crespí had now explored.

There can be no question about the fact that in this particular document it is Verger, and not Father Crespí, who is talking about a map and who has prepared some form of a map. The heading of the document (Chapman #2089, 1772, Dec. 27, Mexico. Antonio Bucareli y Ursua to Julian de Arriaga) : "Acompaña copia de la representacion, Diario y Mapa que le paso el Guardian del Colegio de San Fernando de Mexico correspondiente al nuevo descubrimto. del Puerto de S. Franco. en la Peninsula de Californias." (Microfilm, Bancroft Library, for the "representation," diary, and map, #1936, *AGI*, Aud. de Guad., 512, Roll #111.) The map, unfortunately, has been separated from the #1936 item and appears as item #1842. This *may be* the form prepared by Verger, or prepared for him. It is the form reproduced in this volume, and previously reproduced as the "Crespí" map by Bolton and Harlow (see above, p. 123).

In a Mexican version of the Crespí 1772 diary, not seen by this writer, there is "an explanation and key for a 'figure' that take up the last three pages of the manuscript. The sketch that can be reconstructed from this copious legend is so like the Guardian's map that it must be concluded that his contribution was, at most, to suppress some details. . . . " So states Alan K. Brown in *loc. cit.*, 390–391, footnote 62, above.

If we return to the 1772 expedition itself we find a further bit of information on the matter of a possible Crespí map.When Crespí himself described his return to Monterey on April 5, 1772 he explained that after a short rest he proceeded at once to mission San Carlos de Carmelo to report to Father Junípero Serra. After receiving Serra's blessing "I told him about the journey and what we had discovered, and delivered this diary to him. . ." Four months later, when Serra was writing to Verger (Monterey, 8 August 1772, in Tibesar, *op. cit.*, #22), he explained how he had given instructions to Crespí to "keep an exact diary, and take especial note of directions, latitudes and all details that might prove helpful.

"The good Father carried out his instructions with painstaking care and came back to this his mission on April 5 during the night. The evident result is that, from here, it is impossible to reach the Port of San Francisco by land. *You will see the diary and the map*, and you will understand how and why . . ." (italics, T.E.T.). Father Serra also referred to a Crespí map in July, 1775 (see footnote #66, above) in such a way that he must have been talking about a map of the Bay, but again the term "Crespí" map could mean one prepared by Crespí or by someone else using the Crespí diary.

After his return to Mission San Carlos on the night of April 5, 1772, Father Crespí soon left for San Diego. He had on one occasion expressed a desire to leave the northern area, for climatic reasons, and was now sent by Father Serra to the southern mission where he arrived after an overland trip of one month, on 13 May. About one month after that—6 July 1772—Crespí wrote to Father Verger, stating that he was following the suggestion of the Reverend Father President Palóu of the Lower California missions, by sending his "poor diary" which he had prepared in March (Bolton Papers, Item #91, Folder #92, Alta California). Then follow comments on the results of the expedition, including the statement that the "great River" at the end of the estuary prevented their reaching the "famous port" (of San Francisco). On May 21st, still in San Diego, Crespí wrote to Father Palóu. Again there is comment concerning the expedition but again reference only to a diary, and nothing about a map. Actually, the reference to the diary is a rather curious one. Crespí states that he believed the estuary and the river they had seen had a sufficient depth for large ships. "Upon the which I have to formulate a diary as soon as I can, and I do not know whether this can go with the ship (by which this letter is being sent). If it does not, I will remit it to Your Reverence, that you may send it to the College." (Bolton papers, Item #95, Folder #26, Alta California).

After some months in San Diego Father Crespí returned to Monterey where he arrived on St. Andrew's Day (30 November) aboard the ship, *El Príncipe*. He soon thereafter wrote another letter to Guardian Verger. In this letter of 23 December Crespí stated: "From Mission San Diego I wrote Your Reverence and sent my poorly prepared diary concerning the March expedition in which we discovered the Rio Grande de Nuestro Reverendo Padre San Francisco in the latitude [*altura*] which is expressed in the diary, and which I suppose you have received with the letter which accompanied it." He then discusses a number of geographic facts which are referred to "in the diary." In this particular letter one would especially expect some reference to a map, even a sketch, yet there is no mention of such. (*Ibid.,* Item #91, Folder #1251).

By December, 1772, Guardian Verger had received the materials from Crespí from which he prepared his "representation" for the Viceroy, as above noted, as well as also, probably, another map for his friend, Casafonda, the Spanish minister of state (see text, p. 46, and note 72).

An examination of the language and thoughts expressed in Verger's writings and the language in the "Description" on the map show some similarities. The basic purpose of the map is to show "the most important part of the Bay" as an extension of the Cabrera Bueno Port of San Francisco. Verger constantly emphasized the importance of this inner bay in his writings; Verger is probably the first student of the Bay question to suspect that the inner Bay was a new discovery and different from Cabrera's Port. If the map we now call the "Crespí" map is Verger's work it may be a "mala figura", but it is not a crude piece of work. (See H. R. Wagner, who refers to this map as a rather crude "bird's eye" view of the Bay area from the Contra Costa, above, p. 123.) The map conforms exactly to Verger's understanding of the latitudes given by members of the 1769 expedition (see end of note 21, above) for Pt. Reyes, placed at 37°44′ and Pt. Almejas at 37°35′, and the mouth of the estuary in between.

One or two additional items of confusion should now be added. Father Palóu in his *Historical Memoirs*, III, p. 250–252, stated that when Fages and Crespí during their march found themselves prevented by the estuary and river from "ascending to Point Reyes," they returned to the presido "and reported everything to his Excellency in the diaries, *from which a map was formed of that estuary and harbor* . . ." (italics, T.E.T.).

And in 1776 when Father Pedro Font, the diarist with Anza, was encamped near Mountain Lake on the present San Francisco Presidio grounds, he recorded that: "I occupied myself today in copying the map of the port of San Francisco *which my cousin, Fray Pablo Font, made in Mexico from the data in the diary kept by Fray Juan Crespí in that journey which he made with Captain Fages.*" (Entry for 20 March, 1776, in Bolton, *Anza*, IV, *Font's Complete Diary of the Second Anza Expedition.*") (Italics in the text, T.E.T.]

Would the rather beautiful calligraphy in the map's "Description" have been the work of Fray Pablo Font rather than that of the Guardian? Whoever did make the "Crespí" Map, it is difficult to believe that anyone who had seen the Bay, as Father Crespí had, both in 1769 and 1772, could have drawn it. The map has always presented a strange appearance to those who have looked at the Bay from the various points from which it was seen by Fages and Crespí. One oddity in the map is the row of seven islands fairly regularly spaced, stretching in a line in front of the *boca*, labelled *Yslas pequenas*, the "little islands." The Sevilla Ms (used by Verger) specifically mentions a farallon and "three islands" in front of the mouth; then following the estuary toward the north northwest there are mentioned four other islands. This makes seven, not counting the farallon. Could anyone who had seen Alcatraz, Yerba Buena, Angel, the Marin Islands, Brooks Island, and Red Rock, presuming these to be the seven referred to, line them up on a map no matter how crudely drawn, as they appear on the "Crespí" Map?

In the diaries San Pablo Bay is described as a large round bay which resembles a great lake of about eight leagues extent. In it "we saw an island." The island is not located through any descriptive information in the texts. On the map the bay is *so* round it might have been drawn with a compass, and the island, which had to be placed somewhere since it is mentioned in the diaries, is placed in the bay, but on the wrong side of the entrance to Carquinez Strait if the island mentioned is presumed to be Mare Island.

It is the conclusion of the present writer that the map now known as the "Crespí" Map was made by someone who did the best he could with the descriptions and observations found in the Sevilla Ms and the Mexican Ms cited by Brown; that this person was not Father Juan Crespí, but could have been the Guardian, Father Rafael Verger, or Father Pablo Font, the cousin of the better known Father Pedro Font.

An any rate, the documentation as provided here makes it plain that one cannot take even a map at face value, and some of the mystery about the origin of the map still remains.

COUNCIL OF WAR AND ROYAL EXCHEQUER*
(Mexico, December 16, 1774)

Council of war and royal exchequer ordered called and held today by the Most Excellent Señor Baylio Frey Don Antonio María Bucareli y Ursua, Henestrosa, Laso de la Vega, Villasis y Córdova, Caballero de Gran Cruz and Comendador de la Bobeda de Toro in the Order of San Juan, gentleman of the Chamber of his Majesty with entry; lieutenant-general of his royal armies, viceroy, governor, and captain-general of this New Spain, president of its royal audiencia, superintendent general of the royal exchequer, president of the council of tobaccos, intendant of this branch, and subdelegate-general of the department of maritime mails in said realm, etc.

There were present the gentlemen Don Domingo Valcárcel y Formento, Knight of the Order of Santiago, member of the council of his Majesty in the royal and supreme council of the Indies, deacon of this royal audiencia, auditor general of war, and superintendent general of the royal quicksilver ships; Don Antonio Villa Urrutia, of the council of his Majesty and subdeacon of it, Don Joseph Antonio de Areche, likewise member of the council of his Majesty and the ranking fiscal of said royal audiencia; Don Juan Chrisósthomo de Barroeta, of the council of his Majesty in the department of exchequer, regent of the tribunal and royal audiencia of accounts of this New Spain; Don Ignacio Negreiros, knight of the Order of Santiago, and Don Santiago Abad, both chief accountants of the head table of that royal tribunal; Don Pedro Toral Valdés, accountant; Don Juan Antonio Gutiérrez de Herrera, factor, veedor, and proveedor; and Don Fernando Mesía, treasurer, both royal officials of the real hacienda and the chests of this court; Don Fernando Mangino, accountant-general ad interim of royal tributes; and Don Juan Antonio de Arce y Arroyo, proprietary accountant-general of the royal alcabalas.

An account was given of what was decided in the council held on the 9th of September of the year last past concerning the utility and the desirability of the exploration of the road by way of the Gila and Colorado rivers to the new establishments of San Diego and Monte Rey, in the terms proposed by Captain Don Juan Baptista de Ansa, and which his Majesty deigned to approve in his royal order of the 9th of March of the present year; and keeping in mind the start which in fact this captain

---

* Bolton, *Anza*, V, pp. 249–258.

made from his presidio of Tubac in the province of Sonora for Northern California, by way of these rivers, on the 8th of January, effecting the opening of the road with the soldiers which were furnished him and with the success and advantages which he sets forth in detail in his diary.

Report was also made of his communication of November 17th, in which, in order that the occupation of the Rio de San Francisco which he is to go to accomplish may be effected, he set forth that for the forty soldiers who ought to accompany him on this expedition the people most appropriate are those of the alcaldías of Culiacán, Sinaloa, and Fuerte in the province of Sonora, to instruct whom in the first military rudiments he asked for five soldiers of the presidios of that province, in order that they may serve as sergeants and corporals; and that in order that they may be better equipped and be assisted with everything which they need, there should be sent to them the necessary articles of clothing, since if their pay is sent to them in cash it will only encourage their gambling and prodigality; that to make this journey it is necessary to take soldiers who have knowledge of the country and of the heathen, for which purpose he asks his Excellency to issue the appropriate orders permitting him to take from his presidio ten of those who accompanied him on the previous expedition, which number it will be possible to replace with five of these and five others of the presidio of Terrenate, to which, since they have a hundred soldiers, so small a number of recruits will not be harmful; and, setting forth the time most suitable for this journey, and the provisions which were sufficient for the other expedition, he explains how difficult it is to obtain useful saddle animals in the alcaldías of Culiacán, Sinaloa, and Fuerte, for they can be furnished only by strictly ordering the alcaldes mayores that they shall require the hacendados to exhibit and sell the animals which they have reserved for the services of their haciendas, besides other things which this petition contains.

Account was also given of the superior decree of his Excellency, dated the 28th of November, in which for the increase of the presidio of San Carlos de Monte Rey he declared necessary a lieutenant, a sergeant, and twenty-eight soldiers, so that without weakening its actual forces it will be possible to detach the men necessary for the two new missions projected in the neighborhood of the San Francisco River, where there is to be established a fort which shall be a sign that it is occupied, and a step and beginning for successive establishments, it being necessary to select the lieutenant and the sergeant from the soldiers of the presidios of Sonora and to take from them only the soldiers who voluntarily may wish to go to that domicile, the number not to exceed eight, the twenty others being recruited by the same Captain Don Juan Baptista de Ansa, and delivered by him to the commander Don Fernando Moncada, he assisting in the exploration of the river in order that he may report what he may have seen; and he taking for his return by the same road ten soldiers chosen from his presidio besides those which have been mentioned.

Likewise, report was made of the nominations for lieutenant and sergeant who, Don Juan Baptista de Ansa said in his opinion of the 5th of the present month, must be furnished by the presidios of the province of Sonora, he proposing for the first Don Joseph Joachín Moraga and Don Cayetano Limón, both alféreces, the former of the presidio of Santa Rosa Corodeguachi, and the second of San Carlos de Buenavista; and for sergeant, Don Joseph Ignacio Espinosa, corporal of the first company of the presidio of Terrenate, and he asks that he be permitted to select the ten soldiers which he needs.

Likewise, an account was given of the estimate of the cost of clothing for thirty recruits, men and women, and clothing adequate for one hundred and eighty children, arms, saddle animals, rations, and equipage for the service and transportation of everybody from the province of Hostimuri to the presidio of San Carlos de Monte Rey; cattle, provisions and transportation for these; mess for the commander and chaplain; provisions and aid for the new establishment; and presents of glass beads for the Indians all of which amounts to twenty-one thousand, nine hundred and twenty-seven pesos and two reales, including in this amount the goods possessed by the royal exchequer in this city and in Los Alamos.

And, keeping in mind what was decided in the council of the 8th of July of the year just past, and meditating upon everything with the deliberation appropriate to so important a subject, it was resolved in common accord that for the new expedition or journey which Captain Don Juan Baptista de Ansa is to make from his presidio of San Ignacio de Tubac to that of San Carlos de Monte Rey and the two new missions which are to be established, everything shall be done as he has proposed for the success of so laudable an enterprise. To effect this and for the soldiers which his Excellency estimated necessary to accompany him, there shall be issued by this most excellent gentleman the appropriate commissions of lieutenant and sergeant to one of the persons whom Captain Ansa has proposed for each office. To Ansa's choice shall be left the selection of the ten soldiers which he needs to accompany him, and the rest the same captain shall recruit as he may wish. And his Excellency, for this purpose and to check desertions which they may commit, shall issue to the respective justices the strictest orders to the effect that on their part they shall aid Captain Don Juan Baptista de Ansa in this and other matters which may come before them concerning the accomplishment of this enterprise, until by the same road which he explored he shall deliver the men to commander Don Fernando de Rivera y Moncada.

And he shall assist in the exploration of San Francisco River, in order to be able in consequence to inform his excellency as to what he may see, and shall return with the ten soldiers of his company. And he shall be accompanied as on the first expedition by Father Garcés, who shall await him on the banks of the Colorado River until his return. And besides this father, he shall be accompanied also by Fray Pedro Font on the whole journey in order that, as an expert, he may observe the latitudes. And for this purpose there shall be sent to him by the hand of Captain Ansa the instruments which he may need, the appropriate dispatch being issued by way of charge and entreaty for this purpose by his Excellency to the reverend father guardian.

And, having seen the total of the expense which this expedition will cause, and of which an estimate was made in detail by Don Joseph de Echeveste and the same captain, this royal council reflected upon the matter at great length, and it was decided with regard to the costs that from the Pious Fund destined for the propagation of the faith in the Peninsula of Californias there shall be taken ten thousand pesos of the funds existing in the chest provided for their custody. For this purpose the director shall put in charge of the royal officials of this Court ten thousand pesos for the expenses of the new expedition, delivering them to the factor Don Manuel Ramón de Goya; and they shall do the same with the rest which may be spent for this expedition, and whatever it may be it shall be on account of the royal exchequer; and they shall deliver two thousand dollars more of the same fund to the síndico of the College of San Fernando, one thousand for each of the new missions which are to be established on the San Francisco River or in its vicinity.

It shall also be the duty of his Excellency to issue the appropriate dispatch to the reverend father guardian, in order that for them he may appoint ministers chosen from the fathers who are now in Monte Rey; and ten thousand pesos for expense money for the department of San Blas which, according to the royal council of July 8 of the year just past, they ought to advance for once only from the Pious Fund existing in the said chest and not yet paid. And to provide for the new positions of lieutenant, sergeant, and the other soldiers, the appropriation for the Californias shall be increased.

And finally, with a view to what was represented by Don Juan Baptista de Ansa, to the effect that he was not able personally to gather the provisions of the members of the expedition because he had to embarrass himself with recruiting the new troops in different places, for this purpose his Excellency shall name a person for this task, that is to say, Don Miguel Gregorio de Echarri, who is proposed by this captain, and who it is said managed such affairs with credit in the garrison of Pitic during the military expedition of those provinces, or another person who may be of his choice, he to name the pay which is to be given him for his labor, and the person whom he is pleased to name shall keep an account of what he may spend, to present to the intendant or royal official of Los Alamos.

And for everybody there shall be made certified copies of the costs and of the proceedings of this council, one for the commander Don Fernando Moncada; another for the factor Don Manuel Ramón de Goya; another for the tribunal and royal audiencia of accounts; another for the royal officials of this court; another of the same and of his representations of the 17th of last month and of the 5th of the present month for Captain Don Juan Baptista de Ansa; and this person, the factor Goya, and the commander Moncada, each one separately, and likewise the father ministers, shall keep formal and certified accounts of their respective expenses to sent to his Excellency as soon as their distribution and destination shall be determined.

And finally, a copy in triplicate shall be made in order to give an account to his Majesty of everything newly done up to now, from the royal order of approval henceforward, because this has been done with respect to everything theretofore.

All of which was thus agreed to and signed by the gentlemen who composed the council. Mexico. December 16, 1774.

ANTONIO MARÍA BUCARELY (Rubric); VALCÁRCEL (Rubric); VILLA URRUTIA (Rubric); ARECHE (Rubric); BARROETA (Rubric); NEGREIROS (Rubic); ABAD (Rubric); VALDES (Rubric); GUTIÉRRES (Rubric); MEZÍA (Rubric); MANGINO (Rubric); ARCE (Rubric); JOSEPH DE GORRÁEZ (Rubric). Mexico, December 23, 1774. Let everything decided in the present royal council be put into effect.

ANTONIO MARÍA BUCARELY (Rubric).

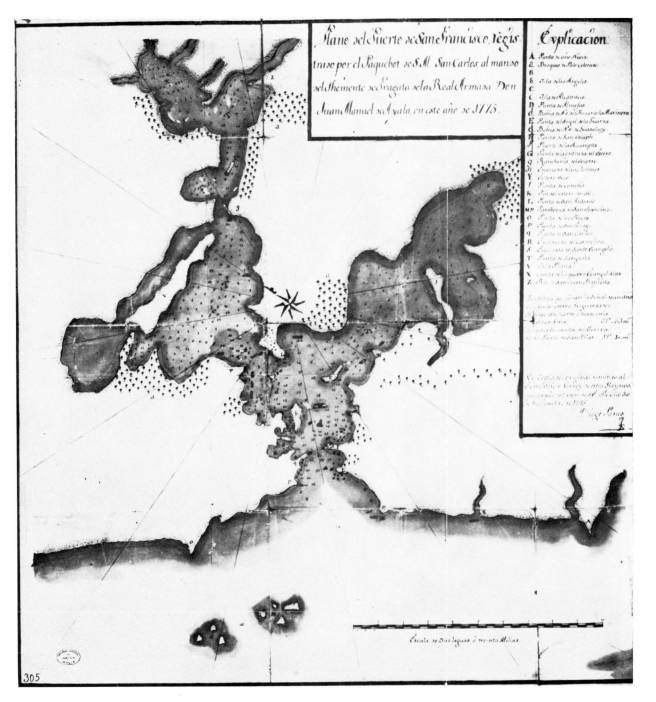

APPENDIX 7

The Ayala Map of San Francisco Bay, 1775.

QUESTIONS CONCERNING THE "FOUNDING OF SAN FRANCISCO" AND THE FOUNDING DATES OF THE PRESIDIO AND MISSION

The student of local history is faced with some interesting problems in deciding on the precise dates for the founding of the presidio and the mission as well as in the interpretation of a broader question—did these establishments constitute the "beginning of San Francisco"?

There can be no doubt that the first encampment in the founding period was made at the future site of the mission. The date of that encampment was 27 June 1776. The next day an *enramada* (arbor) was built and an altar set up in it, and the day after that, the day of St. Peter and St. Paul, both Father Palóu and Fray Pedro Benito Cambón said mass. Father Palóu stated that "we continued saying mass every day of the whole month that we remained at that place" (from D. E. Dane's translation, *CHSQ*, XIV, #2 [June, 1935]).

Moreover, when the main body of people moved to the vicinity of the Presidio site, the two priests, the guard of six soldiers, one or two settlers, the livestock and mission properties remained on the mission site. Father Palóu stressed the nearness of the mission to the Presidio site; he mentioned that he said mass in the first tule hut built at the Presidio site on July 28, two days after the move was made. Obviously, the setting up of an altar for celebration of the mass was a normal operation to which no undue significance need be attached. Also, there seemed to be movement back and forth between the sites, for this was a time of preparation in both areas.

Before the arrival of the much-awaited *San Carlos*, Lieutenant Moraga stated, on August 6, that "one of the soldiers assigned as escort at the mission came to me with the news that about forty armed Indians had arrived near the mission . . . and that they were bound for a village near the mission, whose Indians had wounded one of their companions." In Moraga's account one finds additional references to the mission than the ones mentioned here, all prior to the date of the formal founding of the mission. (Bolton, *Anza*, III, "Moraga's Account.")

It is doubtless necessary to make a clear distinction between the arrival of the Moraga expedition—which was the beginning of continuous residence in the area—and the formal ceremonies of founding which were for the Presidio, the 17th of September, and for the Mission, the

9th of October, both in 1776. In March 1777, after his return to Monterey, Serra wrote to the Viceroy: "In reference to the foundation of the fort, and of the first mission of San Francisco, Our Father, Your Excellency must have heard all about it before me, as I was in San Diego during September and October when these foundations were made." (Tibesar, *op. cit.*, III, #112, Serra to Bucareli, 1 March 1777). Thus, Serra appears to have accepted the same dates provided by Palóu for the founding of the "fort" and then of the mission, September and October, respectively, in 1776.

In formal celebrations, nowadays, to honor the events of the twin foundings, the formal foundation dates would seem to deserve the greatest consideration, especially in view of the air of exultation which is expressed in the words of the original participants. A "founding of San Francisco" celebration, if scheduled in June because the Moraga party had begun its encampment in June, 1776, more or less on the future mission site, does not carry with it the original meaning of the Spanish occupation of the San Francisco Bay region, since the June celebration would reflect an almost exclusively sectarian interest in the mission. Nor would such a celebration give proper honor and consideration to the founders themselves who planned *their* formal celebrations with all the pomp and circumstance which frontier conditions permitted.

Finally, entirely apart from a choice of dates as to when the presidio and mission were "begun," it becomes apparent in succeeding years that neither institution was, except in an indirect and symbolic sense, the foundation for the future city of San Francisco.

An interesting speculation is found in J. N. Bowman, "Determination of the Birthdays of Urban Communities," *CHSQ*, XXVII, #1 (March, 1948). The author asserts flatly: "The mission was founded on June 29, 1776, . . . The church was dedicated on October 9, 1776 [i.e., the church built near the brush arbor] and this, rather than the founding date, appears in the usual lists and is generally accepted as the birthday of the mission. It is the one given by Palóu, and was no doubt used so that the mission might appear to have been founded after the presidio *in accordance with the governor's instructions that no mission was to be founded at the time of the establishment of the garrison*." Dr. Bowman continues: "In the founding of the California missions a common method of procedure was followed; Dolores [*sic*] is the only one whose dedication date was listed as its founding date, even though the "comenzada" date on the title-pages of its parochial books gives August 1, 1776. From its founding on June 29, 1776, the mission continued its history without interruption until secularized in 1834" (italics, T.E.T.). The distinguished Franciscan scholar, Father Maynard Geiger, O.F.M., in his *The Life and Times of Fray Junipero Serra* . . . , II, pp. 140–141, states: "The true date of the founding of Mission San Francisco has long been a matter of dispute. Engelhardt's statement that 'June 29, 1776, five days before the Declaration of Independence, was really the date of the founding of Mission Dolores or San Francisco de Asis, although officially other dates are reported,' simply cannot be maintained. On that basis most of the founding dates of the California missions would have to be changed and would not be in accord with the ideas of the men who founded them. Neither Palóu nor any of his contemporaries ever attached any significance to June 29, 1776, beyond the celebration of Mass on the spot where the *future** mission would arise. The official mission registers, inscribed by Palóu, give the date of founding as August 1, 1776, the day when building operations began without the religious ceremonies usually accompanying the formal founding of a mission. Thereafter, each year in his *extant, original, official reports*,† Palóu always states that the mission was founded on October 9. This is also the date Father Cambón the co-founder, gives during the years he was at San Francisco and during the years after Palóu returned to Mexico. After him, the official annual reports during the whole mission period always give October 9 as the date of founding." Later, in his analysis of "beginnings," Father Geiger states: "Since the present city of San Francisco grew out of the development of the mission, the presidio, and the later Yerba Buena, all three of which grew into one, the date of the beginning of that community stems from the day of the first definitely established place within it. That place was the presidio, formally founded on September 17, 1776" (p. 141).

The interpretations of "beginnings" by John W. Dwinelle provides a curious record of historical attitudes, apparently depending upon circumstances. In his rather famous work, a legal brief, *The Colonial History of the City of San Francisco: being a Narrative argument in the Circuit Court of the United States for the State of California, for Four Square Leagues of Land Claimed by that City and Confirmed to it by that Court* (S. F., Towne & Bacon, 1866), Mr. Dwinelle, after a slightly mixed-up version of the events preceding the San Francisco establishments, declares, *in capital letters* "THE SEVENTEENTH OF SEPTEMBER, A.D. 1776, MUST THEREFORE BE CONSIDERED THE DATE OF THE FOUNDATION OF SAN FRANCISCO." It should be understood that Dwinelle developed the argument that the

---

* Italics, Geiger.
† Italics, T.E.T.

City of San Francisco was entitled to four square leagues because the city had grown out of the Presidio, not out of the Mission. His argument was sustained by the Supreme Court of California in Hart *vs.* Burnett (15 *California*, 530) in the ruling "According to our view the Pueblo of San Francisco was first formed out of the presidio of that name; and not out of the mission."

However, in 1876, during a "Centennial Celebration" (see *Our Centennial Memoir. Founding of the Missions. San Francisco de Assis [sic] in Its Hundredth Year. The Celebration of Its Foundation. Historical Reminiscences of the Missions of California* [San Francisco: Compiled, Printed and Published by P. J. Thomas, No. 505 Clay Street, 1877], when Mr. Dwinelle was one of the honored orators for the occasion, we find him proclaiming exactly the opposite from his contentions during the litigation: " . . . on the 8th day of October, 1776, the pious missionaries planted the Cross at the Mission of Dolores, chanted the first [sic] mass, and consecrated its soil to Christianity and civilization. As they then intended that the Mission which they thus founded should become the future Town, and as they chose that date for the performance of the official act which gave a birth, a name, and a practical existence to our city, we must accept their choice, *and date the anniversary of our foundation from the 8th day of October, 1776* [italics, T.E.T.]. On that day, and by that act, the mission church, the orchards, and the cemetery became the property of the Catholic Church, by a title which is far the oldest title to land in the city; it completes its first century to-day." (It goes almost without saying that Mr. Dwinelle was making his address on the 8th of October, 1876, and that his very words, last quoted, had been the contention of the United States in the litigation referred to above and that during the litigation Dwinelle had supported the founding date of the Presidio as a "birthdate" for San Francisco.)

The Archbishop (Alemany) spoke on the same day, and appears to have provided a less lyrical and more historical approach to San Francisco's background than did the attorney, Mr. Dwinelle. His Grace said, in part: ". . . . today we celebrate the Centennial of the Foundation of this Mission, and of this vast metropolis of the Pacific Coast" and "we are solemnizing today the hundredth anniversary of the existence of San Francisco *as a civil and religious community* [italics, T.E.T.], because we are especially interested in the establishment and prosperous duration of its double edifice, the foundations of which were laid in this place by our forefathers a hundred years ago." (*Our Centennial Memoir*, pp. 59–60.)

"But the Mission of San Francisco was not founded until the 8th day of October, 1776", continued the Archbishop. "Three weeks before—namely, the 17th of the preceding September—the Presidio of this place had been founded with the usual formalities; and, according to the wishes and instructions of the Viceroy of Mexico, the Missionary Fathers, accompanied by the civil authorities of the Presidio, performed the memorable work of the foundation of the Mission with all possible solemnity and formality . . ." (*Ibid.*, p. 62.)

The Archbishop's point of view was clearly that a joint civil and religious community had been founded, beginning with the Presidio and continuing with the Mission.

Another orator on the "Centennial Day" in 1876, was General Mariano Guadalupe Vallejo. The General in his speech provided a very accurate summary of events leading to the founding of both the Presidio and Mission. Vallejo's principal historical contribution to the record was the assertion that although the ceremony of founding for the Mission (4 October, "the very day of our Seraphic Father, Saint Francis") could not be carried out on the Founder's Day owing to the failure of Moraga to return in time from his explorations, in later years the 4th of October was celebrated. He stated, after discussing the question of the 8th *vs.* the 9th of October (which neither the Archbishop nor Dwinelle referred to), that: ". . . it is beyond question that the old Fathers, since my earliest recollection—and, from tradition, I know, before my time—always considered the *fourth of October*, the Feast of the Patron Saint; but would not this rather tend to strengthen my assertion that, having selected a Patron for their Mission, they would *dedicate that day to the celebration* of the foundation? I do not wish to be at variance with the gentlemen who differ with me on those points; but I owe it to myself to maintain what of my own knowledge has been the accepted opinion of those who have long since passed away. The fact of the postponement of the celebration of an event from accidental causes will not change the original intention. The celebration of the anniversary of American Independence, when the 4th of July falls on Sunday, is always held on the Monday following; but it is the *celebration of the Fourth of July*, nevertheless." (Italics, Vallejo.)

Obviously, General Vallejo was unhappy over the choice of the 8th of October date for the 1876 Centennial and wanted it understood that despite the day on which he was speaking *he* was really celebrating the hundredth anniversary of a foundation dated the 4th of October, the Feast of the Patron Saint.

The above comments have to do mainly with the determination of dates, but running through them is the theme of the "founding of San

Index

notes on 38, 47–50, 54, 56, 62, 65, 81, 84, 85, 87.

Cabrera Bueno, Joseph Gónzalez: author of navigation handbook, 13 & n.; description of the "Port of San Francisco," 13; mention, 12 n. 14, 16–17 & n., 22 n., 28 n., 29 n., 31 n., 48, 85, 100.
Cabrillo, Juan Rodríguez: 15 & n.
Calabasas Creek: 83 n.
California Historical Society: ix; and *Quarterly*, ix, 12 n., 89 n.
Cambón, Pedro Benito: comments on Monterey, 45–46; co-founder of San Francisco mission, 65, 88 ff.
Campa [y] Cos, Miguel de la: 74 n.
Cantil Blanco (Fort Point): cross raised by Anza and Font, 82; mention, 25, 68, 72 n., 81 n., 82 n., 85.
Cañizares, José: pilot of the *San Carlos*, 65; enters San Francisco Bay in ship's long-boat, 65 ff.; surveys San Francisco Bay, 66 ff.; his *Ynforme*, 71 n.; mention, 66 n., 68 n.
Carmelita Bay (Richardson Bay): 67.
Carmelo River: 64.
Carquinez Strait: 40, 84.
Casafonda, Manuel Lanz de: 11 n., 45 & n., 46 & n., 47.
Castaic: 87 n.
cayuco: built of native redwood, 64; used in survey of San Francisco Bay, 68, 73; mention, 79.
Cermeño, Sebastián Rodríguez: 12 ff., 13 n., 15 n., 43.
Chapman, Charles Edward: Dedication; ix; 1 n., 23 n., *Catalogue*, 47 n., 48 n., 49 n., 50 n., 51.
Charles III: royal *cédula*, 4 f.; 48–49; mention, 1, 27.
Colorado River: 53 n., 132.
Conmy, Peter T.: 144.
contra costa: 22 n,. 26 & n., 29 & n., 35 f., 84.
Cook, S. F.: 100 n.

Corodeguachi, Santa Rosa (presidio): 131.
Costansó, Miguel: member of San Blas Junta, 1768, 4 f.; *Diary* and *Narrative*, 17 n., 18 n., & ff.; first map of San Francisco Bay, 22 f., 42 f., 66; mention, 16 ff., and notes.
Council(s) of War: 16 May 1768 (San Blas), 4 ff.; Portolá expedition, 11 November 1769 (Palo Alto area), 29 & n.; 9 September 1773 (Mexico), 52 f.; 16 December 1774 (Mexico), 129 ff.
Crespí, Juan: *Diaries*, 39, 41–43 n.; description of San Francisco Bay, 1769, 16 ff., & notes; exploration of the Bay, with Fages, 1772, 39 ff.; comments about the Bay, 40–41; names lower Sacramento-San Joaquin systems, 40.
"Crespí" map of San Francisco Bay: 42, 43 & n., 64 n., 118 ff.
Croix, Carlos Francisco de: orders exploration of San Francisco Bay, 32 n., 37 f., 39, 49 & n., 62 n.; mention, 2 n., 3 n.
Culiacán (*alcaldía*): 130.

Dane, George E.: 90 n.
Davidson, George: 17 n., 36 n.
"defensive expansion" (Spanish Empire): 1 ff., 50 n., 51.
derrota (Cape Mendocino to Acapulco): described by Cabrera Bueno, 13 & n., 105.
Dolores, Arroyo de los: 83–84.
Dolores, Laguna de Nuestra Señora de los: 89 & n.
Dragon (ship): 2.
Drake, Francis: 15 n.
Drake's Bay: 12, 14.
Drake's Estuary: 17 n.
Drewes, Rudolph H.: 42 n.
Dutch: source of concern to Spain, 2 n.
Dwinelle, John W.: 141–42.